MUSICAL INSTRUMENTS OF AFRICA

■ Music is far more important in the life of the African than it is in ours. From the time he is a tiny baby, the African child learns about life through music: legends, tales with a moral, work songs, religious songs.

To accompany their music, Africans use instruments of many kinds — percussion, strings, woodwinds, brasses. They are made from whatever material is at hand: clay, metal, tortoise shells, gourds, bamboo, animal horns, hides, snakeskins, seeds, stones, palm leaves, calabash fruit; roofing metal and empty oil drums if they can be found.

What these instruments are like in Africa south of the Sahara, how they are made, the sounds they produce, and the way they are used form the subject of this book. Photographs show the instruments, some by themselves and others in actual use by the players. Other illustrations include line drawings and the music of African songs. The book also contains lists of phonograph recordings keyed to the text, of books suggested for further reading, and of the nations of Africa.

On an accompanying long-playing record are examples of the music of African instruments.

Colin M. Turnbull, Assistant Curator in charge of African Ethnology at the American Museum of Natural History, New York City, has provided the Introduction. The record accompanying the book is made from tapes that Mr. Turnbull recorded in Africa.

MUSICA

Illustrated by Richard M. Powers

INSTRUMENTS OF AFRICA

Their Nature, Use, and Place in The Life of a Deeply Musical People

BETTY WARNER DIETZ and

MICHAEL BABATUNDE OLATUNJI

The John Day Company ■ New York

Library of Congress Catalogue Card Number: 65-13733
Manufactured in the United States of America
Designed by The Etheredges
Second Impression

To

LESLIE, SUSAN, and BEN WARNER

and

KWAME, FALASHADE, and MODUPE OLATUNJI

ACKNOWLEDGMENTS

■ Special mention of sincere appreciation is made to the following:

COLIN M. TURNBULL who offered invaluable direction and information, provided the authentic African music for the recording which accompanies this book, read and criticized the manuscript, and wrote the Introduction.

LEONARD KENWORTHY for advice and continued moral support, bibliographical assistance.

IRENE VITE for sharing her photographic skills.

LAURA FELLEMAN and NANCY MORRISON, two fifth-graders who read and criticized the manuscript.

SOLOMON ILORI for information about African music and the permission to use his photograph.

AMY OLATUNJI for preparation of bibliography.

MARIAN TILIN who made the African recordings of Columbia Records available for listening.

HUGH TRACEY who provided photographs and technical information.

ED BAGWELL, BERT MILES, and PAUL CORDES for artistic photography.

THE GHANA INFORMATION SERVICES, SOUTH AFRICAN INFORMATION SERVICE, BRITISH INFORMATION SERVICES, UNITED NATIONS, UNESCO, and WIDE WORLD PHOTOS for permission to use their photographs.

The staff of the EAST MEADOW (NEW YORK) PUBLIC LIBRARY who provided equipment, space, and time to listen to their extensive collection of ethnic recordings.

The librarians of the BALDWIN (NEW YORK) PUBLIC LIBRARY, the NEW YORK CITY PUBLIC LIBRARY, the LIBRARY OF CONGRESS, and the INTERNATIONAL LIBRARY OF AFRICAN MUSIC at Roodeport, Transvaal, South Africa, who helped to locate research information and photographs.

The personnel of three museums — THE AMERICAN MUSEUM OF NATURAL HISTORY and the METROPOLITAN MUSEUM OF ART in New York City, and the COMMERCIAL MUSEUM of Philadelphia — for permitting the use of their facilities and libraries and for allowing their photographs to be reproduced.

CONTENTS

INTRODUCTION

■ One of the most encouraging things about the young generation, these days, is perhaps its zest for making music. It may not always please the parental ear or grace the eyes, but the making of music is one of the oldest and most healthy forms of self-expression known to man, and for too long most of us have been mere listeners.

Here is a book that will help those who want to develop new musical skills, and the writers not only suggest new ways of getting new sounds, but also, sometimes inadvertently perhaps, add a new twist to the accompanying body movement called dance. I know that I would like to see what happens to a class of schoolchildren given this as a textbook by an imaginative teacher.

Dr. Dietz and Mr. Olatunji first of all set the place of music in African life, and this is of prime importance. For perhaps the great secret of African music, and the one aspect of that music that was surely brought to this country, is its vital significance and relationship to everyday life. It is a part of life itself . . . so much so that at times it seems almost incidental. But whether it is some tiresome domestic chore that needs lightening, or some encouragement that is wanted in battle, some dispute to settle between two villagers, or some inexpressible thought to express, music, in Africa, is there to fulfill its divers functions. Directly, inspiringly, subtly, incomprehensibly, music makes of man a fuller man.

The writers would be the last to say that this is a definitive work on African Music. It is not intended to be. Their aim has, in my opinion, been not only more realistic but infinitely more worthwhile. It is to give their readers a basis for adventuring into this realm themselves . . . not merely to make noises, not even just to make music, but through making music, and specifically African music, to arrive at a better understanding of the African peoples and cultures.

Ultimately it might even help the reader, young or old, to know himself better. If this happens, then the writers will have more than achieved their goal.

New York, New York

COLIN M. TURNBULL
Curator of African Ethnology,
American Museum of Natural History

MUSIC IN AFRICAN LIFE

■ All Africa sings, dances, and plays musical instruments spontaneously. Music is far more important in the daily life of the African than it is in our lives. Music is part of everyday work, religion, and ceremonies of all sorts. It is even used for communication. Many tribes have no written language, so they send messages by word of mouth, through singing, blowing signal whistles, or by using talking drums which imitate the pitch of the human voice.

The African child learns about life through music. His mother sings to him throughout childhood, even when he is a tiny baby. Through singing and clapping he learns about the members of his family and the important people and events of his community, tribe, and country. His mother sings tales of the famous native drummers and dancers who are considered very important people in Africa. By singing songs which contain a moral, his mother teaches him what his people consider to be right or wrong. As he listens to neighbors singing things they dare not say, he learns even more about what his people value. They quarrel, mock and insult each other, and later make up, all through song.

The child listens to work songs.[1] The singers are farmers, fishermen, hunters, herdsmen, porters, camel drivers, soldiers, or coffee sifters. When brush cutters clear a field for planting rice, musicians entertain and encourage them by playing small slit drums. An agricultural song provides rhythm for work in the fields. Porters carrying African chiefs or Europeans in sedan chairs on long journeys through the bush or forest walk to the rhythm of their singing. In equatorial Africa boatmen and fishermen sing boat songs and paddling songs. Herdboys play flutes as they watch the cattle. In desert areas there is even a song to make the camels drink. Soldiers sing to set the rhythm for their marching. Hunters celebrate a successful hunt with singing and dancing. When the Pygmies kill a male elephant with long tusks the entire village sings and dances for hours. The call-and-response form is common to many of these songs. A leader starts the song, the group answers, the leader sings again and is answered by the group, and so on.

Singing, dancing, hand clapping and the beating of drums are essential to many African ceremonies, including those for birth, death, initiation and famous events.[2] The singing and dancing at marriage ceremonies go on for hours with hundreds of people participating. At African funerals beautiful music is played as a tribute to the deceased, and this last performance is kept as happy as possible. People pay homage to their chiefs and kings[3] with music and dance, and the royal drummers of some tribes even play drum rhythms and melodies on tuned drums as their kings move from home to office. No ceremony is complete without music, but African people sing joyously whether they have a special reason or not.

Music and dance are important to religious expression. The Yoruba tribesmen who worship the god of thunder sing and dance vigorously during the Shango Ritual.[4] The Spirit enters their bodies as they dance to the powerful, complex rhythmic patterns. They are overpowered and sometimes collapse. The religious effect is so great that the dancers expose themselves to fire without danger. They do not feel the fire nor do their bodies show evidence of being burned. The chanting, accompanied by the rhythm of the drums, gongs, and rattles, seems to transform them.

The Pygmy people believe so strongly in the goodness of the forest that one might almost say they worship a forest god. To them the forest is father and mother. If illness or death strikes, or if the hunting on which they depend for life itself is bad, they believe that the forest is sleeping. So they wake it up by singing to it around a great fire, night after night. Colin Turnbull, who lived among the Pygmies for several years, was told,

1.   The numbers throughout refer to specific recordings on which certain types of music may be heard. For instance, work songs may be heard on the records after which the number 1 is written; iron gongs on records with the number 16 (chapter on Idiophones), etc.   See page 109 for recordings.

"We wake [the forest] up by singing to it, and we do this because we want it to awaken happy. Then everything will be well and good again. So when our world is going well then also we sing to the forest because we want it to share our happiness."

The religious music of African Christians and Jews is an intermixture of Western and African music. Ethiopian Jews sing prayers for Passover to the accompaniment of a *masonquo* (lyre), gongs, and drums.[5] Catholics in Ethiopia and in the former Belgian Congo[6] create Masses accompanied by drums and rattles — Masses in the traditional Catholic form, but music adapted from their own ritual songs. And Protestants in West Africa compose hymns based on melodies used in the pagan worship of their ancestors.[7]

Political events are celebrated with music and dance also. Famous persons, native or foreign, are greeted with music when they arrive and saluted with music when they leave. Natives break into spontaneous music and dance at political rallies, elections, town council meetings, and Independence Day celebrations. The African, whether primitive or civilized, makes music an essential part of his daily life.

To some Africans music is magic. They sing songs for rain, for good luck, or to lay a charm on hunters so that no harm will come to them. Songs with clapping are thought to cause healing, and shots are believed to frighten away evil spirits.[8] The spells and prayers of the medicine man which are accompanied by singing and dancing often do produce healing. Modern psychiatrists who recently did research in Africa believe that the witch doctor's suggestions and the wild "possession" dances of some tribes are really ancient methods of curing mental illnesses. Today we call this psychotherapy.

How Africans use their bodies as musical instruments is described in the next chapter. The handiest and best instrument of all is the human voice. Africans are superb singers. The body serves as a drum as people clap hands, slap thighs, pound upper arms or chests, or stamp or shuffle feet. This body percussion creates exciting rhythms which stir folk to action. Wearing rattles or bells on wrists, ankles, arms, and waists increases the emotional response. Some Africans, such as the Pygmies, use few musical instruments other than the voice and body percussion, yet they have achieved a high musical level.

As you read about the musical instruments of Africa, remember that Africa is not a country, but a vast continent nearly four times the size of the United States with a population of about 230 million. Nearly a thousand different languages are spoken in the almost sixty countries. This continent is one of the most varied in the world.

Many people think of Africa as a "dark continent," a land of hot jungles and deserts. Actually, there are only two deserts, the Sahara in the north and the Kalahari in the south. Snow-capped mountains are found a short distance inland from the Mediterranean along the northwest part of the continent and above the high plateaus of the eastern lakes region. On these high plateaus one welcomes the warmth of a blanket all through the summer nights. The grasslands stretch down the east coast to the mountains and plateaus of South Africa. It is here that many of the wild animals are found. The whole of central Africa is covered by a rain forest.

In this land of varied climates and land forms live people of equally great variety. They differ in size, in color, in the ways they live, and in the values they hold. Therefore, it should not surprise us to learn that their musical instruments differ somewhat according to the environment in which they live.

Africans make musical instruments from the materials they find around them. In forest areas they make large wooden drums. Elsewhere drums are made of clay, metal, tortoise shells, or gourds. Some tribes have no drums. Where materials are scarce, as in the savanna, few instruments are used. Singing is accompanied mainly by body percussion. Xylophones are made of lumber or bamboo. Flutes are found wherever reeds or bamboo grow. Animal horns become trumpets. Animal hides, lizard skins, and snakeskins are used as decoration and provide the membranes for drumheads. Laces made of hides and skins fasten together parts of instruments. Hide strips become the strings of harps, fiddles, and lutes. Bamboo may form the tongues of thumb pianos, the frames of stringed instruments, and stamping tubes. Strips of bamboo are even clashed together rhythmically. Gourds, seeds, stones, shells, palm leaves, and the hard-shelled fruit of the calabash tree are made into rattles. Ancient Africans even made musical instruments from human skulls decorated with human hair. Modern Africans use waste materials such as strips of roofing metal, empty oil drums, and tin cans. These people, bursting with rhythm, make music with everything and anything.

This book contains information about the musical instruments of Africa south of the Sahara. Those of the north will be described in a separate volume, to be called *The Musical Instruments of the Middle East,* for the music of Islam is far different from the music of the rest of Africa. The instruments are grouped according to the classifications often used by anthropologists and musicologists. Those which we call *percussion* instruments are classified as *membranophones* and *idiophones*. The *membranophones* have vibrating membranes and include many forms of drums. The *idiophones* include the rattles, xylophones, rasps, and slit-log drums — instruments whose entire bodies vibrate to produce sound. Our *brasses* and *woodwinds* are classified as *aerophones* — instruments which enclose a body of vibrating air. Our *strings* are classified as *chordophones* — instruments which produce sound through the vibration of strings.

BODY PERCUSSION

■   Everywhere in Africa songs and rhythmic accompaniment are inseparable. The African sings, chants, and imitates instruments with mouth sounds.[9] He uses his body to create percussive accompaniments for his singing and dancing. Everyone is a composer, for participation in musical activities is spontaneous. The mother picks up a crying baby to calm him with her singing and she is calmed, also. First she sings a vigorous song, moving rhythmically with the baby on her shoulder or in her arms. Next she sings a soothing lullaby[10] and, as the baby relaxes, she puts him down and goes about her work. When the baby grows older he imitates his mother's singing. When a new baby arrives, the older child creates songs to sing to him, just as his mother did. Since no music is written (not even the Catholic Mass mentioned earlier), the child need not "learn" music. Following the example of the adults around him, he composes his own melodies and rhythms. Thus Africans acquire their music.

The African uses his entire body as an instrument to provide rhythmic accompaniment for his dancing. He makes percussive sounds with hands, feet, and mouth. He slaps his chest, thighs, knees, arms, and hands. Stamping dances are common everywhere, but especially where drums are scarce, as among the Nguni people of South Africa. The old war songs and dances which once accompanied tribal fighting are rarely performed.

Yet, on days of great importance, hundreds of men gather together to engage in ceremonial singing and dancing, shaking the earth with their rhythmic stamping.

You can use your body as a percussive instrument, too. Master the variations described here, then compose new rhythmic patterns, for creation is better than imitation. This kind of participation will develop your ability *to hear* and *to feel* the complex rhythmic patterns in the recorded music of Africa — rhythms which otherwise might escape you.

VARIATIONS

■ 1. Sing a familiar song. Clap in time. Clap every beat first, then every other beat. Clap only the accented beats next. Develop syncopation. After clapping each of the types of rhythm through an entire verse of your song, divide the class into two or more groups and clap several versions simultaneously.

■ 2. Stamp your feet, changing the rhythm from time to time. Add clapping in a different rhythm. Then add tongue clacking. Later imitate drums, rattles, and other instruments with mouth sounds.

■ 3. Stamping dances are important throughout Africa. They may be solo or group dances. Sometimes the groups move in a circle, sometimes they dance in line formation. The dancers choose some symbolism to guide their dance creation. Forest folk may portray a leopard, pastoral people may depict a cow, or hunters may show their respect for the mighty elephant. Since ancestor worship is common in Africa, a dancer sometimes selects an animal, bird, or tree which appears on his family totem.

Imagine yourself a Masai herder living in East Africa. Stretch your arms outward and upward to depict cow horns. Then do the following stamping dance.

Begin the six-count dance pattern by standing with your weight on the right foot. Place the left foot forward (count 1), then backward and slightly to the left (count 2). Stamp as you bring the left foot to the right one, transferring your weight (count 3). Standing firmly on your left foot, place the right one forward (count 4). Stamp as you step right, changing weight again. Stamp as you bring the left foot to the right one, but do *not* shift your weight (count 6). With your weight firmly on your right foot, you are ready to repeat the entire variation over and over, moving to the right in a circle.

Do some steps of your own creation while leaning forward with your arms stretched straight backward. Another time, bend low, stretching your arms forward as if you were about to throw yourself on the ground. Then choose your own symbolism and develop more complex patterns.

■ 4. As you sing, clap hands (count 1), slap chest left (count 2), slap chest right (count 3), and tap open mouth (count 4). Repeat again and again. Increase your speed as you gain skill. Notice changes in voice resonance as you tap your open mouth while singing.

■ 5. Sit on a chair. Slap both knees simultaneously (count 1), clap hands (count 2), stamp both feet while making percussive sounds with your mouth (count 3, count 4). When you can do this capably, double the speed and the actions — slap knees twice as fast (count 1 and), clap hands twice (count 2 and), etc. Devise new combinations in this sitting position.

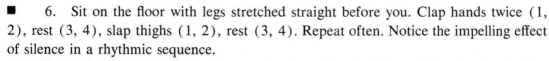

■ 6. Sit on the floor with legs stretched straight before you. Clap hands twice (1, 2), rest (3, 4), slap thighs (1, 2), rest (3, 4). Repeat often. Notice the impelling effect of silence in a rhythmic sequence.

■ 7. Cross your legs while sitting on the floor. Slap both knees (1), clap hands (2), slap right knee with right hand (3), slap left knee with left hand (4), and repeat. Devise new patterns of clapping hands and slapping knees.

■ 8. Spread your legs wide. Increase speed to establish a brisk tempo for the next variation. Clap hands twice, slap thighs twice, clap once, rest one count, slap thighs once, rest one count. Repeat as rapidly as you can.

■   9.   Slap the floor between your legs, using open palms (1, 2), clap hands (3), slap thighs (4), and add mouth percussion to any or all of these counts.

■ 10. Create rhythmic patterns while kneeling. Use some of the variations above.

■   11.   Stand up. Beat your chest to create rhythmic accompaniment to your singing. Begin with a slow series of chest slaps (1, 2, 3, 4). Double the speed (1 and 2 and 3 and 4 and). Do this several times. Next beat a fast 6/8 time in this manner, accenting the counts underlined (1, 2, 3, 4, 5, 6). Later hum or sing while beating your chest vigorously. Note differences in voice resonance. Another time tap your foot on the accented beats while you do the variations suggested.

■   12.   Learn to sing *Menu Di-yeh*. Sing this African song as you beat your chest and tap your foot.

■ 13. Now you are ready for a more difficult type of body percussion. Place your left arm across your chest with your hand under the right armpit. Keep your left hand relaxed so that your fingers can beat a rhythm in this position. Cup your right hand and place it on top of your bare left arm above the elbow. The arm must be bare to produce the proper sound. Slap hard in time to your singing. Tap regular beats with the fingers of the left hand and slap your arm sharply with your right hand just *before* each beat. Notice the difference in sound created by *tapping* with the fingers of one hand and *slapping* with the other.

■ 14. Beat 6/8 time with the fingers of your left hand (1, 2, 3, 4, 5, 6) and slap your cupped right hand on 1 and 4. Later add foot tapping in any rhythmic pattern you wish.

You, too, can make music without real instruments. Be as ingenious as the Africans are.

MEMBRANOPHONES

■ Drums are basic to the African orchestra. Those which have vibrating drumheads (or membranes) are described in this chapter. Those whose entire bodies vibrate when struck are described in the next chapter.

Large batteries of drums are played together in forest regions, but hand clapping, stamping, and rattle shaking take their place where there are no natural forests. At Lake Matuba the natives make drums of earthenware with snakeskin heads which are covered with reed mesh. In Liberia a women's secret society uses a drum made of a tortoise shell. Elsewhere drums are made of gourds. Thus we see that drums are made of varied materials.

Contrasting pitches are necessary to every good orchestra. Therefore, drums of different sizes and pitches are used together in drum batteries. Some drums have fixed pitch, others can be tuned. The Yoruba of Nigeria have three types of drum batteries — the *igbin* drums, the *dundun* or *gangan* drums, and the *bata* drums. In Kenya the *efumbu,* a long drum, and two smaller drums called *endonyi* are played together. Square and round drums comprise the *atenesu* battery. In Uganda the Entenga Royal Drummers of the Ganda tribe play sets of *entenga* tuned conical laced drums, and the Nyoro tribesmen play batteries of *ntimbo* drums which look like water urns.[11]

The drum is a symbol of power in many African tribes. Among the Tutsi tribe of Rwanda no one other than the Mwami (chief) and the Queen Mother may have sets of drums. Drummers have high status and the position of master drummer often is inherited. Sons of master drummers are taught their skills at an early age and spend their entire lives perfecting their art.

Examine carefully the pictures which follow in order to learn for what purposes drums are used, how they are played, and of what they are made.

■   Natives of the Kingdom of Burundi beat out the message of independence on tribal drums as the former Belgian-administered United Nations Trust Territory of Ruanda-Urundi became two independent nations on July 1, 1962. The gay singing and dancing were followed by silence as the Belgian flag was lowered. Shouts of joy filled the air as the Burundi flag of red, white, and green with a drum on it was raised. The celebration which followed included more singing and dancing and the parade in which these drummers participated. Their drums vary in size and shape, and thus in pitch. Each man plays his drum with two sticks as he balances it on his head with only a pad of cloth for support and protection.

Wide World

British Information Services

■   When Princess Margaret of Great Britain visited Kenya, she was welcomed in the traditional manner. Here we see her admiring a beautifully decorated *efumbu,* a long drum which is held by the leader of the dance team which welcomed her. With the aid of Sir Evelyn Baring, the Governor of Kenya (beyond her), who acts as her interpreter, she inquires about the drum. She learns that it has a single head of animal skin and that it is open on the bottom. The *efumbu* is played with two smaller drums called *endonyi*. Three drummers can create rhythms of great complexity on these three instruments whose different pitches can be heard clearly.

■ At a gold mine near Johannesburg, South Africa, a Bantu drummer (either a Zulu or a Xhosa of the Nguni nation) plays a homemade drum for his fellow gold miners. It appears to be a single-headed drum made from a garbage can or other discarded metal container. Drums are scarce in South Africa. The Zulu people once used their hide shields as drums, and both the Zulu and Xhosa people used stiff oxhides called *ingqonqo* as temporary drums in ceremonies.

South African Information Service

■   Traditional drums are seen in this picture of children dancing to the rhythm of a Venda orchestra at a kraal in the Sibasa District of the Northern Transvaal, South Africa. The large drum, *ngoma,* is made from a section of the trunk of a marula tree over which an oxhide is stretched. Its single head is pegged in place and is beaten with a stick by either men or women. This drum is played only by the Venda people and is used for ceremonies. The taller, conical drums, *murumbu,* have single heads pegged in place. Notice that the women hold these drums tightly with their legs as they play them with their hands. Both drums are played with or without the Venda reed-flute ensembles. The *murumbu* is similar to the *moropa* which is played by the Transvaal Sotho people.

■ The *sakara,* pictured next, is easy to make. It is nothing more than a clay circle covered with goat hide. The picture shows its bottom side to illustrate the details of construction. The top looks like a tom-tom. Make a circle of clay, like a tire, and push out a rim about one-half inch high on the top. The circle may be any size, but twelve inches in diameter is common. Fire the clay. Stretch wet animal hide across the top, tuck it in around the rim, and fasten it with sharply pointed pegs while the hide is still wet. Allow the drumhead to dry thoroughly. The pegs seen here are of bamboo but wood could be used. Purchase a damaged drumhead from a musical instrument concern, for goat hide may be a bit hard to obtain.

To play the drum, hold it close to the left side of your chest with your left hand. Place your thumb under the rim and your four fingers on the drumhead. Press and release to create rhythm while your right hand beats a second rhythm with a wooden beater. Note that the handle of the beater is wrapped with cloth. This drum is common to Liberia and Nigeria.

From Olatunji collection of African instruments   *Bagwell and Miles*

■ Everybody loves Saturday night! Here we see revelers in a public square in
Conakry, Guinea. The drummer in the foreground is playing a *tambour,* a double-
headed drum just like the Nigerian *bembe.* The other drummers are playing *conga*
drums held between their knees. Notice that the *tambour* is played with two drumsticks
while the *conga* drums are played with the hands.

So popular is revelry on Saturday nights that West Africans sing a song about it,
each nationality in its own language.   Here it is in Yoruba, a Nigerian language, and
English.

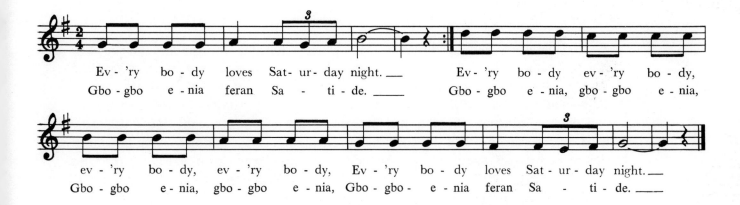

Ev - 'ry   bo - dy   loves   Sat - ur - day   night. __   Ev - 'ry   bo - dy   ev - 'ry   bo - dy,
Gbo - gbo   e - nia   feran   Sa - ti - de. ____   Gbo - gbo   e - nia,   gbo - gbo   e - nia,

ev - 'ry   bo - dy,   ev - 'ry   bo - dy,   Ev - 'ry   bo - dy   loves   Sat - ur - day   night. __
Gbo - gbo   e - nia,   gbo - gbo   e - nia,   Gbo - gbo - e - nia   feran   Sa - ti - de. ____

■   Babatunde Olatunji illustrates the manner of playing a *conga* drum which is typical of drums used throughout West Africa. With his left hand he plays the down beat in the center of the drum. He follows this with a slap on the side of the drum with his right hand. He creates different pitches and resonances by varying the use of his hands and fingers. Sometimes he uses the fingertips of one hand to strike the side of the drumhead and repeats this with the other hand. Then he makes a roll by striking the fingertips of both hands alternately on the side of the drumhead or up and down from the middle to the tip of the drum. Then he holds the hands at the outside rim of the drumhead. Elbows are used, also. Olatunji slides his left elbow from the center of the drum to the rim while beating the drumhead rapidly with the fingers of his right hand. Why not try these effects on your drum?

■   Talking drums capture our imagination. To us it seems impossible that drums can be used to send messages. Yet they imitate tonal languages such as Ewe, Yoruba, Ashanti, Kongo, Kele, Swahili, Ngala, Ibo, and Bechuana so clearly that natives have no difficulty in understanding the ideas communicated. Drums with skin tops are used in pairs, one drum giving a low tone and the other giving a high tone. Africans, however, do not use these terms. They speak of the gentleness or forcefulness of tones, or say that the drums speak "big" tones or "little" tones. Slit drums, all-wooden drums without skin heads which are described in the next chapter, can be used, too.

   Talking drums are used as telephones and telegraphs. All kinds of messages are sent — to announce births, deaths, and marriages; sporting events, dances, and initiation ceremonies; government messages, and war. Sometimes the drums carry gossip or

Ghana Information Services

jokes. The Ewe people believe that the drums can carry messages to the spirit world after the death of a loved one. When the villages are quiet early in the morning or late in the evening is the best time to send messages. The sounds travel six to seven miles at night, but only four to five miles during the day when the hot air currents carry the sounds upward into the sky. By relaying the messages from drummer to drummer, they can be sent one hundred miles or more. Learning to play messages on drums is extremely difficult; therefore, this art is fast disappearing from Africa.

Agbadga, Ghana's talking drum, is a pedestal drum which is carved from a mahogany tree. The circumference of the bottom part of the drum is smaller than that at the top. The drum is single-headed and is tipped forward to lean against braces when played so that the open end is free. The goatskin or cowhide drumhead is fastened to the drum with hoops, cords, and pegs. Musicians tune these instruments by pounding the pegs to tighten the drumheads and thus raise their pitch. One of the drums pictured is tuned high, one low. The wooden beaters have curved heads.

■   The *kihembe ngoma* of East Africa is one of the most picturesque drums of Africa. Two of the many sizes in which this drum is made are pictured here. Cylindrical in shape, each drum is carved from a tree trunk. Each has two drumheads fastened by means of tightly stretched strings made of gut or fiber. Both the drumheads and the strings may be highly decorative. Can you imagine the beauty of a drumhead made of zebra skin? Picture in your mind the varied designs African artists could create in the lacing alone.

The musician can play the drum, standing it on either its large or its small drumhead. If he wishes to play two pitches on the same drum, he lays the drum on its side and plays both ends. Tapping the large end produces "big" sounds and tapping the small end produces "little" sounds. Whole sets of these drums are sometimes played together, thus

From Olatunji collection of African instruments   Bagwell and Miles

producing a wide variety of pitches. Sometimes a musician straps three small *kihembe ngoma* together and holds them on his knee, playing these alternately with larger drums.

■   Nigeria's talking drums are the *bata* battery, the *igbin* battery, and the *dundun* or *gangan* battery.[12] These drums are used for ceremonies and entertainment, the *bata* drums being used especially for religious music.

Five drums make up the *bata* set, three of which are double-headed cone-shaped drums, and two of which are shallow hemispherical drums with a single drumhead. The three pictured here are the *iya-ilu* (the mother drum),[13] the *omele,* and the *kudi,* named in order of size from largest to smallest. The body of each drum is made of wood encircled with strips of cane. A narrow center portion usually is undecorated. The two heads of different size and tone are fastened together with strips of cane or leather fastened tightly against the body of the drum. This gives them fixed pitch. This *iya-ilu* is gaily decorated, also, with small, cast brass bells which jingle as the drum is played. The musician plays these cone-shaped drums suspended from the neck so that both heads may be played with drumsticks. Each drum produces two pitches.

The two hemispherical drums of the *bata* set are called the *omele-ako* (the male drum) and *omele-abo* (the female drum). They are alike except that the male drum is the larger of the two. These drums are carved from wood and are hollow inside. There is one drumhead made of animal hide fastened with pegs, but the bottom of the drum is solid wood. Cloth rope is fastened around the rim of the drum and leather thong is laced from top to bottom. The black spot on the *omele-ako* pictured here is a spot of tar which affects the tone quality of the drum. The musician hangs this drum from a strap around his neck and plays it with beaters made of twisted leather. The drumheads of the *iya-ilu* and the *omele-ako* are about the same size. Along the Ivory Coast there is a similar drum called a *tabala.*

Bagwell and Miles

American Museum of Natural History

35

Solomon Ilori

■   There are five drums to the *dundun* or *gangan* drum choir. Four of these are hour-glass-shaped pressure drums and one is a shallow hemispherical drum. From largest to smallest, they are the *dundun, kerikeri, gugudu, gangan,* and *kanango.* The *gugudu* looks something like the *omele-ako.* It has a single head of fixed pitch, is worn on the chest suspended from a strap around the musician's neck, and is beaten with leather straps held in each hand.

   Study the photograph of Solomon Gbadegesin Ilori. Notice that he suspends the *dundun* from a wide strap across his left shoulder. He tucks the drum under his left arm, alternately squeezing and relaxing the arm pressure on the leather thongs to raise or to lower the pitch. With his right hand he strikes the upper drumhead with a drumstick shaped like a crane's bill. He can play a melody of almost an octave in range on this drum. The *kerikeri* and *gangan* are smaller versions of the *dundun.*

Notice the details of construction. The drum has thin, tanned goatskin heads at each end which are joined by means of special leather thongs. In order to protect the delicate skins from the vigorous beating, each drumhead is made of two layers of hide, skin on skin. Sometimes brass bells are sewn around the edges of both drumheads for adornment and to provide special sound effects. The bells are classified as idiophones, which are described in the next chapter.

In addition to sending messages with the *dundun* battery, professional musicians play traditional music on these drums. When serving in the private band of a tribal chief, they herald the approach of a visitor with the music of this battery.

■   The *igbin* drum choir played by the Yoruba of Nigeria consists of three drums known as *iya igbin, jagba,* and *epele.* The *iya igbin,* which is the largest, is played with one stick and the fingers, palm, and fist of the other hand. The others are played with two sticks each. These thick, squatty drums with single drumheads sit up on three legs carved out of the bottom of the drum. The bottom ends are open.

The Ghanaian orchestra pictured next has five drums, one *axatse,* and one *atoke* which produce music of widely varying tones and pitches. It consists of three sections — the drum section, the background rhythm section, and the song section. The people who dance will add singing and clapping. The third musician from the left and the one

Ghana Information Services

on the far right illustrate how the *dundun* or *gangan* drums are played. The hourglass shape of the drum is clearly visible. The drummer on the left plays a *bembe,* a double-headed drum of fixed pitch which hangs from his neck as he beats both drumheads with curved-neck beaters. The fourth musician plays two large *conga* drums with his hands. The first and fifth musicians play idiophones, the one on the left shaking a rattle called a *shekere* in Nigeria and an *axatse* in Ghana where this picture was taken. Rattles of this kind are common all over Africa although they may be larger or smaller than the one shown here and may have different kinds of outside nets to produce the rattling sound. The fifth musician taps the *atoke,* a double-headed iron gong which produces tones of different pitches.

Professional musicians in Ghana perform with still another drum battery, called the *asiwui* set. *Atsimevu,* the master drum, is tall and lean in shape, reaching higher than a man's shoulder. *Sogo* is smaller, and *kidi* is the smallest of the three. All are single-headed drums, open on the bottom. Made from strips of mahogany cut to size, they are fastened together with native glue and tacked into elongated barrel shapes. Iron bands then are slipped into place over the tacks. The animal-skin drumheads are sewn to a wooden hoop with thick homemade cord. Loops of cord are tied from the hoop to the drum pegs which are held by friction in the holes bored in the sides of the drums. To visualize this kind of drumhead, look back at the picture of the *agbadga*. The fourth drum of the *asiwui* battery, *kaganj,* is carved from a tree trunk. Its shape is similar to that of the *agbadga,* for it is a pedestal drum. Its head, however, differs from that of the *agbadga* in that the membrane comes down below the tuning pegs where the skin is fastened to a hoop.

The pitches of the four drums vary not only because of their size but also because of the tension applied through tuning. Each of the drumheads is tuned by wetting. The drummer turns each drum upside down, pours in about two glasses of water, and leaves the drum to soak. Then he rolls it on its side to wet the holes into which the drum pegs have been set. This swells the wood. After a short time, he taps the pegs and the rim of the drumhead and tests for pitch. In this manner, a suitable range of pitches may be achieved. When played, the master drum is leaned against a stand so that its bottom end is free. The others are played as they sit on the floor.

Recordings have captured for us the magnificent playing of professional African drummers. Listen to the *igbin, dundun,* and *bata* drums of the Yoruba of Nigeria, the Royal Watusi Drums, the Royal Drums of the Abatutsi, and the Royal Drums of Rwanda to hear what splendid music drum choirs can achieve.[14]

The six single-headed Congolese drums illustrated next are of special interest because of their artistic beauty. Two of the drums are in the form of a human body. The first, a fetish drum, is a realistic figure of a man holding a child on his knees. Seated on a leopard, the man supports a cask-shaped drum on his head. The second is less realistic in form, but one can visualize a long torso, long arms, an oversized head, and very short legs. The band of fine beadwork which encircles the drumhead cannot be distinguished in this photograph. The next three drums are notable for their carved and painted designs. The brown and white ornamentation adds charm to the long, cylindrical wooden bodies. All are carved from tree trunks and have solid bottoms. Notice that there is a hole near the bottom of each to add to the instrument's resonance.

The xylophone in the lower left corner and the rattles at the upper right are idiophones, the classification to be discussed in the next chapter. Native to the southeast coast of Africa, xylophones have found their way into West Africa as well. This one has fifteen slats, each with its own gourd resonator. The musician hangs it from his neck or waist and plays it with two rubber-knobbed beaters.

The largest rattle pictured here, made from a gourd decorated with small shells

Metropolitan Museum of Art, The Crosby Brown Collection of Musical Instruments, 1889

and fringed cord, is held in the player's hands. The other two rattles are worn as necklaces, adding their percussive sounds as the wearer dances. The shorter necklace consists of large cowrie shells, each about two and one-half inches long, strung on woven plant fiber. The longer necklace, five feet six inches long, is made of cocoons attached to a strip of tanned monkey hide. The Zulus of Natal fashioned this ingenious rattle. A dancer often wears rattles and bells of varied kinds on his wrists, ankles, neck, and waist, thus creating his own rhythmic accompaniment.

IDIOPHONES

■ Instruments whose bodies vibrate to produce sound when struck or shaken are called idiophones. In our orchestras and bands they are called percussion. These instruments form the all-important background rhythm section in African music. Among the idiophones are percussion beams, slit-log drums (also called slit gongs), bells, metal gongs, rattles, clapping sticks, thumb pianos, and xylophones. A range of pitches is desirable in the idiophone section as well as in the membranophone section of the African orchestra.

Percussion beams are nothing more than logs laid across the ground. Played by one or more men with beaters, they are used to send messages and to provide rhythm for singing and dancing.

Slit gongs — wooden drums without drumheads — are common in Africa wherever there are forests. These signal drums[15] are carved from mahogany or ebony. They may be any length, from about two feet long to the length of a huge tree. Two wide slits are visible at the top of five of the slit gongs illustrated. The sixth has three slits running the full length of the log. The log is hollowed out inside by carving or burning through these slits. If you look very closely, you will notice a narrower slit which crosses the center portion from one wide slit to another. The wood beneath this section is carved so that one side or "cheek" is thinner than the other in order to produce a high tone on one side and a low tone on the other. The quality of the wood determines the quality of the sound and the size of the log determines the depth of the pitch. Some tribes use whole orchestras of these slit gongs, some being so large that the drummer can sit on the middle. In Nigeria, slit gongs are called *ogororo*.

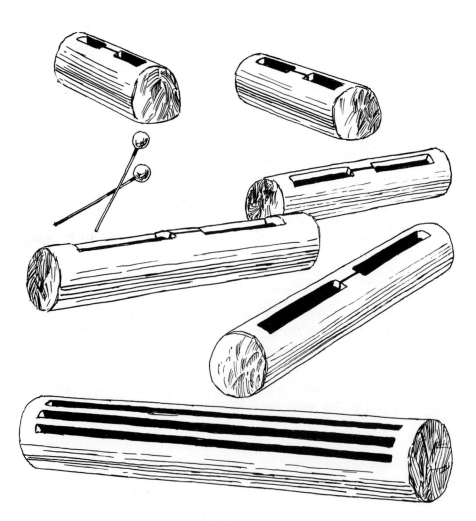

■   Many slit gongs are works of art. This elaborately carved animal, made by members of the Arambo tribe of the northern Congo, is about three feet long. Notice the legs, tail, and the beautiful head of the animal, and the interesting geometric designs on his body. Slit gongs like this sometimes are huge, so big that a man can "ride" the animal as he plays.

Gong-gongs are used as the foundation of the orchestra's background rhythm section throughout Africa. The clink of iron may be used to accompany singing with or without drums, but the iron gong[16] is very important to the drum-dance orchestra. The gong player follows the tempo set by the master drummer and maintains an even beat which the participants match with their clapping. Two gongs usually are used in a dance orchestra, but sometimes as many as sixteen lend rhythmic pulse of differing pitches. Funerals employ four to six gongs.

Some gongs are single and some are double. The West African *gankogui* is a double, clapperless iron gong which is joined together at the top. The player beats the two parts with a stick, producing different pitches as the parts are struck. Many designs other than those illustrated are known, some beautifully decorated. Double gongs of this type are used by carriers in Senegal to announce their approach to a village.

Metropolitan Museum of Art,
The Crosby Brown Collection of Musical Instruments, 1889

■ Africans always make music with the materials at hand. Any metal or bottle may be used as a gong-gong. In the next photograph we see schoolboys playing a bush knife, the *omuhoro,* which is indispensable for cutting paths through thick bamboo forests. Bemba tribesmen of Northern Rhodesia play ax blades in a similar fashion. The tall boy to the right plays the *omuhoro* above his head, striking it with another piece of metal, while the boy directly behind him plays one at chest height. The two drums in the picture are *kihembe ngoma,* more picturesque examples of which were seen in the previous chapter. Notice that the boy on the left carries the drum on his shoulder while the boy behind him beats it with sticks. The boy in the center beats his own drum which is suspended from a strap around his neck.

British Information Services

The xylophone was originally an Asian instrument. It was carried across Madagascar to Africa. From Africa it has spread to the Americas and Europe, where it is used in symphony orchestras and by native musicians, as well.

Xylophones vary in type and size. Some are merely wooden slats laid across two felled trees.[17] Others are more complex. The Nyoro tribe of Uganda plays a *ntara xylophone* which has sixteen tones, sixteen logs not fastened together. Luba tribesmen of the southern Congo play *malimbe xylophones* of two kinds — male and female — each having its bars of wood fastened to a frame. The *malume* (male) xylophone has fifteen bars and the *makaji* (female) has nine bars. Some xylophones have resonators like the one pictured next, others have none. Some of the instruments are large and others are small enough to be carried by means of a cord hung around the player's neck.

The xylophone in this photograph is known as a *yayatsena* in Ghana. Its fourteen bars of wood vary in length to create differences in pitch. Supported on a wooden frame, each bar has its own gourd resonator hanging beneath. The gourds vary in size also, the largest hanging beneath the longest bar. Plant fibers secure the various parts of the instrument. The player taps the bars with beaters wound with rubber, leather, or cloth strips. The drummer in this picture plays the *agbadga,* a drum which was described in the previous chapter. Two *agbadgas* of different pitches may be used as talking drums.

Ghana Information Services

■ Xylophones[18] are used in Liberia, Nigeria, Senegal, and other African countries in a wide band from the west coast almost to the Nile River, as well as in Ghana. They are found also on the west coast, in the southern Congo, in Mozambique, and in the Malagasy Republic (formerly Madagascar). Large xylophone ensembles are used in West Africa and on the southern end of Mozambique. The Chopi tribe of Mozambique are said to be exceptionally fine performers. In Equatorial Africa an ensemble of five xylophones is called a timbili orchestra.[19]

This photograph shows a group of gold miners enjoying a recreational period at a mine near Johannesburg, South Africa. Notice the safety helmets worn by two of the musicians. This ensemble of three *marimba* xylophones is made up of treble, alto, and bass instruments. Notice the width of the bars on each instrument and see if you can tell which man is playing the xylophone with the lowest pitch. Notice, also, the large drum made of a discarded oil container. Remember, South Africa has few forests. Therefore, they make drums of whatever materials they can find.

You may find it interesting to note the varied clothing worn by the miners. Some are attired in European clothing. One of the players is barefooted, wears a European T-shirt, and native clothing below the waist. In the right foreground, we see one man's leg, indicating that he is wearing native clothing except for a pair of European shoes.

The thumb piano, a finger xylophone, is native to Africa and is common throughout the continent. It is known nowhere else except in parts of the Americas where it was taken by Negroes. If you study the nine thumb pianos illustrated, you will notice that each has a number of metal or rattan tongues attached to a sounding board or box. Sometimes an additional resonator is used to increase the instrument's volume. Each tongue is a simple idiophone which the player strikes to produce a soft sound like that of a xylophone but with more of a plucked tone quality. There may be as few as eight tongues or as many as thirty-six. Metal pieces or shells may be hung onto the board or its handle to add rattling sounds of a different quality. While most thumb pianos are rectangular in shape, they may be any shape. Notice the beautifully decorated triangular sound box at the lower right. The attractive designs on these instruments reflect the African's innate artistic sense.

The many names given to this instrument throughout Africa are interesting. Known as a *sansa*[20] or *zanza* in Equatorial Africa and West Africa, it is called a *kembe* in Central Africa. In Nyasaland it is known as a *mbira*[21] and the Zezura tribe calls it a *mbira huru*. The *mbira* name is common — in Tanganyika the instrument is known as the *malimbe mbira*. Near Elisabethville in the Congo it is called the *chisanza mbira*, and in Southern Rhodesia it is called the *kalimbe mbira*, the *njara mbira*, and the *shona mbira*. In the Congo and in parts of Tanganyika it is known as the *lukembe*[22] and in Nigeria it is called the *agidibo*. In other parts of Africa it is called the *kaffir* piano, the *kasayi*, the *maduimba*, the *insimbi*, the *oopoochawa*, the *kisanji*, and the *eleke*.

From Olatunji collection of African instruments   *Bagwell and Miles*

■   The *ilukere,* made of a horse's tail, may be considered a musical instrument, for it makes a swishing sound when waved gently and a whistling sound when whipped briskly. Used all over Africa, dancers wave it to indicate when a dance pattern is to be changed, thus using it as a sign of leadership or authority. It may also set the pace for singing or dancing. A chief employs the *ilukere* as a signal. The complete horses' tails have colorful handles wrapped with leather and wound with leather thongs. If more than one person in a group carries an *ilukere,* the one used by the leader must be thicker, of a different color, or more heavily ornamented.

■ Rattles,[23] the commonest of all idiophones, are found throughout Africa. They are made of whatever materials are available — gourds, seashells, tin, basketry, animal hoofs, horn, wood, metal bells, cocoons, palm kernels, or tortoise shells. These rattling vessels may be single objects containing jingling substances, groups of several rattling objects joined, or rattles which are suspended in such a fashion that they will hit another object. Rattles may be shaken in the hands or worn as belts, leg bracelets, arm bracelets, or necklaces. If worn, the shells, bells, cocoons, or other materials are suspended from leather or fiber strips.

Gourd rattles[24] appear in many sizes. The *agbe* (Nigerian) or *lilolo* (Congolese) is one of the largest. The gourd of the calabash tree is cut while the lid is wet and the seeds are cleaned out. After being thoroughly dried in the sun, the gourd is covered with a net made of string. Colorful beads, strips of bamboo, or cowrie shells woven into the loose net strike the gourd to create rattling sounds when the instrument is tapped or shaken. Because the hollow gourd acts as a resonator, this is one of the loudest rattles in all Africa.

Babatunde Olatunji demonstrates the proper way to play the *agbe*. He places the neck of the gourd in the palm of his right hand and supports the round bottom with his left palm as he taps the instrument. Sometimes he tosses the *agbe* from one hand to the other, holds it with both hands and shakes it, or taps it upside down, as in the second picture. The cowrie shells on the net of this instrument make a beautiful rattling sound. Special coordination and skill are needed to play this instrument.

Only professional musicians are permitted to own and to play the *agbe*. Each instrument is made for a specific musician. The *agbe* never is loaned, not even to other musicians within the same family. A son who is a professional musician, however, may inherit his father's *agbe*.

Olatunji collection of African instruments   **Bagwell and Miles**   *From Olatunji collection of African instruments*   **Bagwell and Miles**

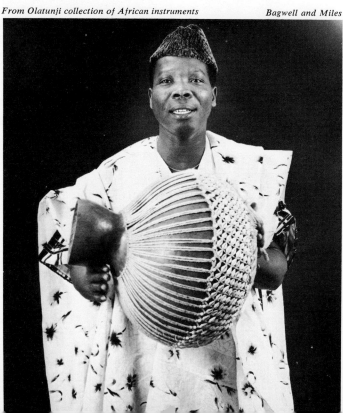

From Olatunji collection of African instruments   *Paul Cordes*

■   The *shekere* held by this beautiful Nigerian dancer is made from a gourd which is smaller than the calabash. It, too, is covered with a woven net. Its brightly colored beads create a loud sound as they strike the resonating hollow gourd. Used throughout Africa south of the Sahara, this instrument is known by varied names. In Ghana, where it is known as the *axatse,* short lengths of bamboo may be woven into the net instead of beads. The *axatse* usually accompanies the *gankogui* as an important part of the background rhythm section of a Ghanaian orchestra. You may wish to look again at the orchestra picture in the previous chapter.

From Olatunji collection of African instruments   *Bagwell and Miles*

■   The *shawaro,* an artistically decorated tin rattle, may be played singly or in pairs. They may be held in any position. Kwame Olatunji shakes a pair as he holds them upright. Seeds, stones, or beads, enclosed within the rattle, jingle pleasantly when shaken.

■   Spontaneous music and dance are common in the lives of Africans. This dance took place in the village of Awandjelo just south of Lama-Kara in Togoland in April of 1958 when the people elected a new Chamber of Deputies to replace the former Legislative Assembly. A few moments after the completion of a campaign speech, the crowd gathered and began to dance. Both the woven shell leg rattles worn by the dancers and the clapping sticks they carry are idiophones. The jingle of the shells, the sound of the clapping sticks,[27] and the throbbing of drums in the background provide rhythm for their gay singing and dancing.

The Pygmies accompany their singing with clapping sticks, also. The very hard wood from which their sticks are made produces a hollow sound.[28] During the honey season the Pygmies stop hunting wild game and spend their time searching for honey trees. There are special dances and songs for this season of which one, the honey song, is accompanied by these sticks.

■ The seven-foot-tall Watusi tribesmen perform tribal dances to the accompaniment of no fewer than eighty different instruments. The major emphasis is on rhythmic movement. Their dances demonstrate the graceful movements of the various parts of the body and require extraordinary skill to perform. In this spear dance the rhythm is provided by a *kihembe ngoma* and the ankle rattles worn by each dancer. The rattles[29] consist of brass bells attached to leather strips. The Watusi live in Uganda and Rwanda, Burundi, but since independence resulted in uprisings, the Red Cross is aiding them to resettle in Kivu Province, the Congo.

British Information Services

This dancer is wearing ankle and waist rattles made of the hoofs of small animals. Notice how they are suspended from a belt woven of fiber so that they swing freely and strike against each other as he dances. Around his neck he wears a rattling necklace made of bamboo. Some pieces of bamboo are left long, and some are fashioned into beads. The metal *shawaro* he holds in his hands probably is filled with seeds or small pebbles.

Sometimes dancers wear anklets, bracelets, and waist rattles made of metal bells. If they are of varied sizes they tinkle in different pitches, thus creating pleasant sounds to emphasize the rhythm of the dance.

From Olatunji collection of African instruments   *Ed Bagwell*

Rattles and bells (idiophones), and flutes and a whistle (aerophones) are seen next. The five rattles in the top row are made of reed-fiber wickerware filled with seeds, stones, or shells. One rattle has a base made of a piece of calabash. Another has a head made of animal skin. Wickerware rattles may be of any size, from tiny ones to those as much as six feet tall.

The gaily decorated flute and four wooden bells with wooden clappers in the second row are beautifully carved and painted. The *ngonge* at the far right is attached to a dog's collar so that his master may be able to hear exactly where he is as he herds animals into an enclosure.

The Metropolitan Museum of Art, The Crosby Brown Collection of Musical Instruments, 1889

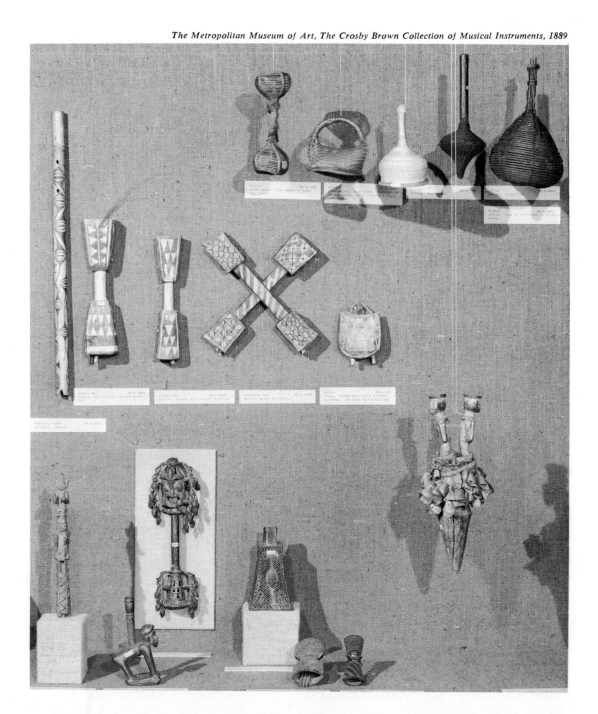

A unique rattle hangs to the far right just below the second row of instruments. Carved of wood, its handles consist of two human figures. The hoofs of small animals, suspended from fiber cord, create a rattling sound when the object is struck or shaken.

In the bottom row, from left to right, we see an intricately carved wooden flute, a metal whistle in the shape of an animal, two metal bells, one with rattling objects attached, and two wooden bells. Notice the great beauty of the art work on these instruments. The two flutes and the whistle serve as a transition to the next chapter in which aerophones are described.

AEROPHONES

■ Aerophones — instruments which enclose a body of vibrating air — are the wood-winds of the African orchestra. In the lowlands, grasslands, and forests, whistles and flutes are made of wood, bamboo, clay, and horn. Trumpets and horns — which are equivalent to the brasses in our orchestras — are made from the tusks of the elephants of the rain forests and from the horns and tusks of the buffaloes, antelopes, elands, gazelles, and the many other animals which roam the grasslands. Wood and gourds are fashioned into trumpets, also. Some are called singing gourds.[30] The skins and hides of snakes, crocodiles, zebras, leopards, and other animals are used for decoration, and the shapes of animals provide inspiration for design. Along the seashore, shells are made into trumpets. Ornamentation of wire, brass, and copper appears in the Congo, South Africa, along the west coast, and in other parts of Africa.

Many African tribes have no wind instruments at all and among the tribes south of the Sahara only whistles, flutes, and trumpets are common. The reed instruments found in the Moslem countries of North Africa are almost totally absent elsewhere. A few oboes are found in Kenya, and the *siwa,* a huge bassoon of black wood at least five feet long, is known only on the east coast.

The whistles[31] found throughout the continent are used singly or in groups. Small signal whistles are used by the cattle herders of the South, and in Upper Volta, Wara tribesmen combine whistles of different pitches and sizes to make a band which plays for agricultural and initiation rituals.[32]

These instruments may be plain in shape and design or they may be highly ornamental. The carved wooden whistle seen at the end of the last chapter is an example of one which is beautifully designed and artistically executed. Fashioned of dark wood, its creator carved it into the shape of an ape. Other whistles of this type are decorated with incised lines — that is, lines which are cut deeply into wood. If the wood is dark the lines may be painted white. If the wood is light in color the lines may be stained brown.

Whistles may be made of materials other than wood. Short pieces of horn serve as whistles and often have a short tube inserted into the mouthpiece. Tribesmen of East Africa use metal whistles as battle signals. Clay can be molded into whistles of many shapes and forms and then baked. Pottery whistles shaped in the form of a head similar to the Aztec whistles of Central America and Mexico are not uncommon. Even pottery jars are made into whistling jars like the one illustrated.

Flutes also may be used singly,[33] in pairs, with other instruments of the orchestra, or groups of them may comprise an entire native orchestra. The delicate music of a single flute often accompanies singing. Melodious flute duets are played by the Dogon tribe of Sudan. Ganda tribesmen serve in an orchestra of *ndere* notched flutes which, before independence, played special concerts for the Kabaka (king) of Uganda. Entire sets of stopped flutes, each one playing but one tone, are used by the Amba people of Uganda, the Bushmen and Hottentots of South Africa, and the Pygmies of the Congo rain forests. To play a melody the musicians take turns, each playing his flute at the proper time. This is called "hoquet technique."[34] Some African musicians are sufficiently skilled to play polyphony on these single-toned flutes. That is, they create harmony which consists of two separate melodies played simultaneously. When the flutes are not in use they are stored in their own basket.

Flutes are tube-shaped or cone-shaped and may be end-blown or side-blown. Vertical (end-blown) flutes and transverse (side-blown) flutes are made of wood, bamboo, swamp reed, the stalk of a plant, or a piece of bark stripped whole off a branch. They may be open at the end or stopped. Some flutes are very short, some are very long. The Kiga people of Uganda play flutes which are three to four feet long. Flutes may play one tone each or many tones, depending upon the number of holes and the fingering. In the Lake Victoria region of Kenya, some of the vertical bamboo flutes are tuned to play semitones.

The artistic talents of the native African are evident as one views the various types of tubular flutes. Some are notched, some have ornamental cuffs of brass or copper wire, some have tassels of goat's hair or other material, and some are decorated with zigzag patterns or other attractive designs burned into their surfaces like the one at the right.

The Korekore boy of Southern Rhodesia plays a wooden flute called a *nyere* which is closed at both ends. Side-blown, it has four finger holes, three under the fingers of the boy's right hand and one in the middle of the flute under his left hand. The flutes of other countries are varied and have many different names. In Dahomey one bamboo flute is called an *azoey*. In the Malagasy Republic a six-holed vertical flute is called a *chebab* and a seven-holed flute is called a *djouwak*. In Rwanda a four-holed flute is called an *umuguri*.

The Metropolitan Museum of Art, The Crosby Brown Collection of Musical Instruments, 1889

Copyright by Hugh Tracey, Director, International Library of African Music

■ Modern Africa combines the old and the new. In this picture we see young boys marching in the morning lineup on their way to a village school in the Republic of Cameroon. Some are playing native side-blown flutes and others are shaking gourd rattles. Two boys are playing a modern non-African drum and a pair of cymbals. Music is very much a part of daily life.

Cone-shaped flutes are made of clay, gourds, animal horns, seed shells, or wood. These are played singly to accompany singing, with other orchestral instruments, or in matched sets similar to the tube-shaped flutes. For instance, the Lango people of Uganda play one set of five animal-horn flutes with three stops on the surface and a solid tip, and another set of five clay flutes. In Nyasaland, Chewa tribesmen make *Malipenga singing gourds*[30] which are from four inches to two feet long. Some of the wooden cone flutes are covered with animal hide. Decorations include wide cuffs of plaited leather thongs and ornamental tails of animal hair attached with a piece of woven fiber or leather thong.

Ocarinas are globular flutes. They are made from gourd tips or from the seed shell of an Oncoba in East Africa.

Panpipes[35] are known all over Africa. These instruments have worldwide distribution. Used by the ancient Greeks, they spread all over the eastern hemisphere, into Africa, and into the western part of South America. They look like a group of tubular end-blown flutes bound together with strips of fiber. The number of bamboo pipes varies from two to almost any number, twelve to twenty pipes being common.

Here we see two tribesmen from Katanga in the southern Congo playing *mishiba panpipes*. Each player in the panpipe ensemble plays from two to six pipes. The number of players in the ensemble varies, also, three being a common size group. This photograph shows clearly the difference in the size of bamboo used to make the pipes, the manner in which they are secured by means of plant fiber, and the way in which they are played. Notice the position of the players' lips.

■ Horns and trumpets, found almost everywhere in Africa, are commonly made from the tusks and horns of animals. They are picturesque in appearance, for some are straight, some are curved, and still others are twisted. Some are smooth like most of those illustrated, but some are roughly ridged. The instruments are end-blown or side-blown and range in size from the small signal whistles of the southern cattle herders to the large ivory horns of the tribal chiefs of the interior. They may be much longer or shorter than the ones pictured. The largest one seen here is made from an elephant's tusk which is five feet four inches long. The Mangbetu tribesmen of the Congo have carved ivory trumpets[37] which range from twelve inches to eight feet in length.

Wooden trumpets may be simple in form or as artistically carved as the large one at the bottom of the photograph. Almost three feet in length, this crocodile's head was carved from a solid block of wood and stained black. Bits of glass were added to make the eyes shine realistically.

Notice how the trumpets are decorated. The three on the right, made of ivory tusks, are beautified by staining and polishing. Bands of snakeskin and leather, cords, and tassels ornament two of the clear white ivory tusks. Occasionally wickerwork or bands of metal or wire (not pictured here) add decorative charm. Sometimes geometric designs are incised into the burned surface of a horn, such as that pictured on the left. However, some instruments are completely plain, their shape alone being sufficient to give them beauty. Note the interesting shape of the twisted antelope horn on the left.

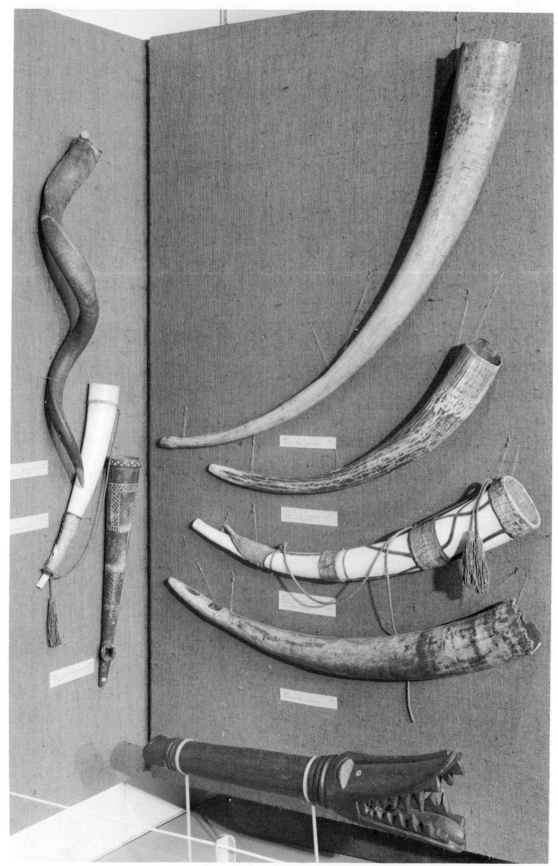

Metropolitan Museum of Art, The Crosby Brown Collection of Musical Instruments, 1889

■   Artistic carving ornaments some of the ivory tusks. Three of these beautiful trumpets from Zanzibar have handsomely carved bands at their large ends. The one which is completely decorated includes in its design two coats of arms and an inscription. This was carved by skillful native artisans under Spanish supervision in the sixteenth century.

■   Other trumpets and horns are made from bamboo tubes with metal bell ends, gourds, bamboo and gourds combined, or conch shells like the one pictured below. This one is called an *antsiva* in the Malagasy Republic. Any gourd may be made into a trumpet by cutting a mouthpiece into its side after the seeds have been removed. Tribesmen of Uganda make a trumpet called the *asukusuk* by attaching a small gourd to a mouthpiece fashioned from a hollow tube of reed or wood by means of fiber cord. The design of the *mare* is the reverse of this, for the mouthpiece is cut into the side of the gourd and the tube acts as a resonator. The *uluru* is made from a larger gourd with a tubular mouthpiece. The *olwet,* made of bamboo and gourd, appears to be an imitation of a European bugle. Similar trumpets are found among the Bantu tribesmen of Rhodesia.

■ Trumpets have a variety of uses, many of which are ceremonial in nature. Musicians play them to herald the arrival or departure of important guests. In religion and witchcraft, trumpets are absolutely necessary. Some tribes believe that their sounds have magic powers which frighten away evil spirits, cure diseases, and protect warriors and hunters from harm. The skins and skulls cf rodents may be attached to these magic trumpets with thong or fiber cord.

These Endo tribesmen were photographed at an Ngoma (dance) in the village of Tot in the Rift Valley of Kenya. Wearing the traditional leopard skin, feather headgear, earrings, bracelets, and beaded necklaces or collars, they listen as their leader sounds the fur-covered trumpet in his right hand while holding another trumpet, made of a curved horn, in his left hand. Notice that the spear dancer kneeling directly behind the leader is wearing a leg rattle made of shells. This spear dance is accompanied by the music of the *kihembe ngoma* (drums) in addition to the rhythmic jingle of the rattles.

British Information Services

British Information Services

◗   When Princess Margaret of Great Britain arrived in Tanganyika to attend the Chagga Council of 1956, a traditional welcome was sounded on this handsome *baragumu* made of the twisted horn of an antelope. The Masai tribesmen of Kenya use similar horns in initiation ceremonies.

◼   These graceful *kakaki* herald the ceremonial departure of the members of a United Nations mission as they leave the palace of the Emir of Dikwa at Bama in the British Cameroons in 1958. Mr. Benjamin Gerig of the United States, chairman of the mission, and the Emir are on the left. Appointed by the Trusteeship Council of the United Nations, this mission went to West Africa to study developments in the British and French Cameroons and to determine which methods of consultation should be adopted when their political future was to be decided. The period of colonialism was drawing rapidly to an end. The Republic of Cameroon attained its independence January 1, 1960.

Kakaki have a beautiful tone quality. Made of long tubes of bamboo capped with copper bell-shaped ends, they are played like our bugle in that the shape of the player's mouth determines the pitch of the tone blown. *Kakaki* are known in other West African countries, as well. A similar trumpet of Cameroon, not as long nor as thin as the *kakaki,* is covered halfway with hide and halfway with snakeskin.

CHORDOPHONES

■   African chordophones — instruments which produce sound through the vibrations of their strings — are divided into three groups: those whose strings are plucked, those whose strings are struck, and those whose strings are bowed.

Musical bows* are of all three types. Of ancient origin, they are pictured in the rock paintings found by archaeologists, the scientists who study ancient life. Simple forms of musical bows are common in South Africa where these are almost the only chordophones known. Farther north along the west coast the bows appear in greater variety and in more complex forms. Some bows have resonators of gourd, calabash, or old tin cans. Others are resonated by the performer when he places the bow against his open mouth. Musical bows are played singly or in pairs.

*   The word "bow" is used in two ways: (1) a bow is a musical instrument, and (2) a bow is used to rub or scrape the strings of a musical instrument, as a violin is played with a bow.

CHORDOPHONES WHOSE STRINGS ARE PLUCKED

The instruments whose strings are plucked are divided into three groups also: harps, lutes, and zithers. There are varieties of each of these, as well.

Harps

The earliest harp was bow-shaped. Later it evolved into a triangular-shaped instrument which is held upright and played with the fingers. Sometimes two sides of the triangle are formed by firm supports with the strings making the third side. Sometimes all three sides of the triangle are of wood — two supports and a crossbar to which the strings are attached. Even today each of these types of harp is played by men somewhere in the world.

The simplest and most primitive harp is the musical bow,[38] which some musicologists** believe to be the ancestor of all stringed instruments. The early African hunter probably discovered the musical qualities of his hunting bow by accident and later improved upon its tone quality by providing a resonator and making other changes, some of which are described in the section on chordophones whose strings are struck. These are classified as dulcimer-type chordophones. If the string is bowed (like the *gubo* of the South African Bushmen or the *chizambe friction bow* of the Karanga tribesmen of Southern Rhodesia), the musical bow is classified as a viol-type chordophone. If the string is plucked, the instrument is classified as a harp-type chordophone.

Some harp-type musical bows are ground bows or pit harps.[39] These consist of a hole in the ground, a piece of flexible wood, and a piece of cord. Perhaps half a gourd is added for resonance. The long, flat piece of wood is driven firmly into the ground and the gourd is buried in the pit. The string is stretched tightly from the upper end of the stick to the gourd. The musician plucks the taut string to accompany his singing. Sometimes the half gourd is not buried. The performer then holds it very tightly under his knee, flat side down, so that the cord places enough tension on the wood to bend it into the shape of a hunting bow.

A more advanced form of ground bow is made from a log, half a gourd, a flat piece of wood, and cord. The wooden strip is driven firmly into one end of the log and the half gourd is fastened to the log about two feet away from the wooden strip. The cord, fastened from the wooden strip to the gourd, is stretched so tightly that the strip bends into the shape of a bow. The player holds the instrument on the ground by placing one leg across the log between the resonating gourd and the wooden strip.

** A musicologist investigates the art of music, studying it in relation to its development and its folk sources as well as its cultural attainments.

The Plateau Tonga tribesmen of Northern Rhodesia play double bows. Two bent sticks, one straight stick, some cord, and an old washbasin are all this Tonga girl needs to make an instrument. Her knees press down on the straight stick which, in turn, presses the bowed sticks firmly against the washbasin resonator. One end of each bow is held firmly against her chest. The bow played with the left hand is used as a drone, producing a single tone. On the other bow, stopped with her chin, the girl plays three tones. She accompanies her song with these four tones.

Copyright by Hugh Tracey, Director, International Library of African Music

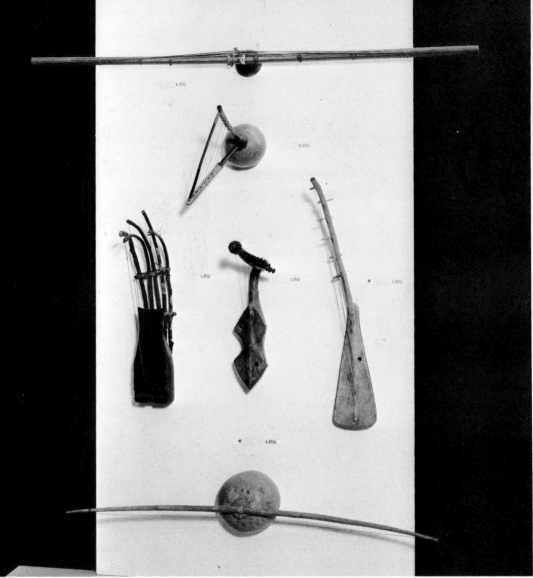

■   To discover how the musical bow may have developed into a harp, study the above illustration carefully. The instrument at the bottom is a single musical bow with a gourd resonator. The one above it to the left is a *pluriare,* a multiple musical bow, mounted on a sounding box. The strings on both these instruments are attached to materials which bend so easily that it is almost impossible to keep them in tune. A string maintains its pitch most effectively when it is stretched tightly.

Several instruments with firm bars appear to be the next stage in the development of the harp. The strings of the *muet* at the top are part of the stiff stalk of a palm tree, and the fiber strings of the *obah* below it are wound tightly around the two wooden uprights fastened firmly into a gourd. The two arched harps to the right of the *pluriare* have firm bodies and firm necks. One additional refinement has been added. There are now tuning pegs along the neck of each instrument by means of which the strings may be loosened or tightened, thus producing the pitch desired. These instruments are shown in greater detail and are described more fully in the pages which follow.

■ Three groups of similar instruments, the *muets, tzetzes,* and *obahs,* appear in this photograph. Played by Fan tribesmen of the Congo, the *muets* (3528 and 1467) are made from the stalks of palm trees. The strings, created by raising strips of bark from the stalk itself, pass over a high, notched bridge in the center of each instrument. Movable loops of fiber cord, wrapped around the stalk and one or more of the strings, regulate the tension of the strings and control the pitch of the music. One *muet* has three gourd resonators like the *vina* of India and the other has but one. To see how a player holds the center gourd against her chest, see the picture of the Zulu girl which appears later in this chapter.

The first, third, and fifth instruments in the bottom row (429, 1492, and 517) are known as the *tzetze, zeze, lokanga voatava, yatta yatta,* or *hova guitar* along the southeast coast of Africa and in the Malagasy Republic. The instrument in the center (1492) has but one wire string. Made of the inverted half of a coconut shell, its 11½-inch carved wood crossbar is held in place by an upright piece of bamboo. The other two

75

instruments have double-gourd resonators. The two gourds are laid one upon the other and attached to the carved wooden neck. A single string made of raffia palm fiber is stretched along one side of the crossbar and doubled back. The *tzetze* on the left has two strings fashioned in this manner and the *herrauou* on the right has three. One of the strings acts as a drone, producing a continuous, low murmuring sound while the melody is played on the other string(s). The performer places the inverted coconut shell or gourd against his chest as he plays.

The two remaining instruments have triangular frames of wood with one corner inserted into a gourd whose open bottom is held against the player's body. Sometimes referred to as a "forked harp," it has many names on the west coast. Even in Sierra Leone there are at least three. Troubah tribesmen call it an *obah,* Cru tribesmen call it a *kanih,* and Sarracolet tribesmen call it a *gambareh.*

■   Lyres,[40] common in Kenya, Uganda, Ethiopia, and the Nilotic Sudan, are almost unknown south of the lake region. The two pictured in the upper half of the next photograph are called *kissars.* The bodies of these instruments are made of calabash. Sometimes they are made of wooden bowls or turtle shells across which membranes of animal hide, snakeskin, or lizard skin are stretched. Each *kissar* has two uprights of animal horn or wood between which a crossbar is fastened. Since the uprights of these two *kissars* are made of horn, they are called *kinandas.* Gut strings are stretched from the body of the instrument to its crossbar. Although some *kissars* have tuning pegs, the strings of these are merely wound around the crossbars. The instruments are decorated with animal tails, tufts of bristle, shark's teeth, cowrie shells (which jingle and act as idiophones), ostrich feathers, fur, bands of leather interwoven with narrow strips of metal, geometric designs scratched into the body of the instrument or similar designs burned into the membrane.

The attractively designed instruments in the lower half of the photograph are arched harps, called *ombis* or *n'goms.* Each has a rectangular body carved from a single block of wood. These resonator boxes are covered with hide which has fur on it, the one on the left having the hide laced clear around the bottom with string. The decorations are carved, the one on the right being covered with arrowhead designs. *Ombis* and *n'goms* are played in Uganda, Kenya, the Congo, and neighboring countries.

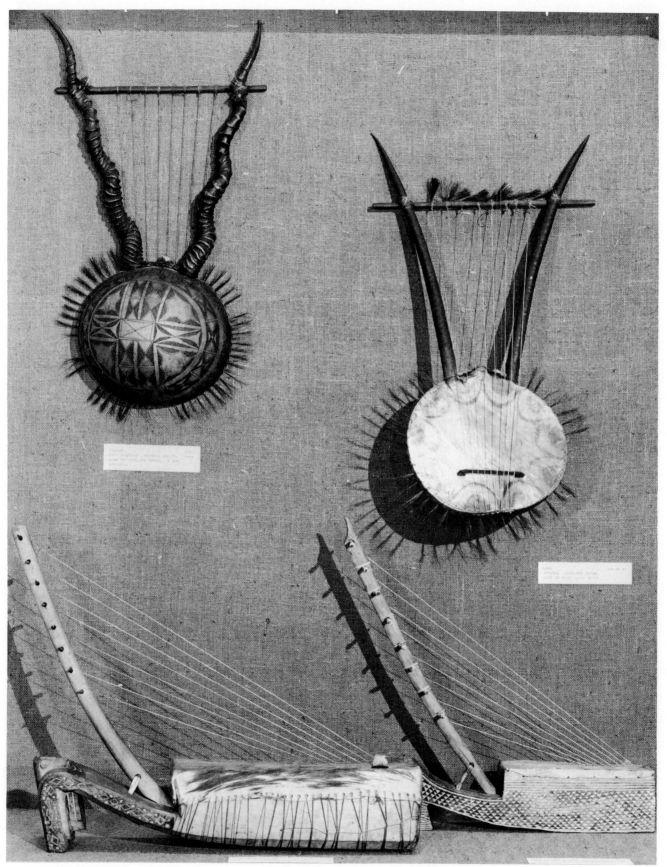

The Metropolitan Museum of Art, The Crosby Brown Collection of Musical Instruments, 1889

■ Apparently Africans have made musical instruments from the materials around them for many, many generations. In the days when there were frequent tribal wars, they even made *kissars* from the skulls of their enemies! These instruments are decorated with human hair and the one on the right has, in addition, a large shark's tooth above the victim's forehead. These Central African *kissars* are museum pieces — relics of a bygone age. The first one is called a *kinanda* because its uprights are made of animal horn. The other two, with uprights of wood, are called *kissars*.

The arched harps in the lower part of the photograph differ from the *ombis* and *n'goms* seen on the preceding page. These are multiple musical bows (*pluriare*). Called the *valga, akam,* and *colangee,* they are played by the Fan tribesmen of Gabon and the Congo Republic (Brazzaville). The *valga* is very much like the *wambee* of Senegal on the west coast. Its body of wood is flat on front and back, and its curved sides taper toward the top. A soundboard is fastened to the body with strips of bark or fiber. The rods at the back, bound to crossbars of wood, are separated slightly. A string is strung from each rod to the bottom of the body of the instrument, and a tin rattle (an idiophone) has been fastened to the upper end of each rod to enhance the sound of the instrument. The *akam's* string tension is regulated by small movable loops of fiber. Its decorations of woven fiber and those of the *colangee* on the right are colorful and attractive. The triangular sounding box of the *colangee* is covered with designs of lines burned into its surface. *Kundi, kasso,* and *angra ocwena* are other names for this kind of instrument. All these instruments are played for personal pleasure.

Arched harps may be played vertically or horizontally, as is illustrated in the next two photographs. Temusewo Mukasa of the Ganda tribe of Uganda plays the *ennanga* (horizontal) *harp*. This is an eight-stringed arched harp with tuning pegs. Its body is made from a single block of wood. Similar in construction to the ancient Egyptian shoulder harps, its neck is curved more gently than those of the *ombis* and *n'goms* pictured previously. There are usually one or two sound holes, and the strings are made from the tail of a giraffe or from animal gut. Other tribes call this instrument a *nanga*. Notice the huge *madinda xylophone,* part of which is visible in the left side of the picture.

Monganika, a Zande tribesman of northern Congo, shows us how he plays the *ombi,* a vertical harp. This instrument also is carved from a block of wood. Its five strings are fastened to five tuning pegs. Monganika wears the local festive clothing, with headdress, bark-cloth breeches, beads, and leg rattles made of seed pods. Can you imagine the jingles you would hear if he were to dance for us?

■ Local musicians greet visiting United Nations officials at Mbe. Republic of Cameroon. The men are playing eight-stringed arched harps. These instruments have wooden bodies, tops made of animal hide, and strings made either of stripped animal hide or plant fiber. Notice that the fingers of the left hand press the string to set the pitch while the right hand holds a plectrum with which the strings are stroked. This instrument usually is played in a minor key.

■ Olatunji demonstrates the proper way to hold and play the harp guitar called a *corah* or *kora*[42] in Guinea, Senegal, the Ivory Coast, Nigeria, and other west coast countries. He rests the end peg against his body as he plucks the strings with his thumbs and forefingers, holding the instrument by its two protruding round wooden sticks. Other names for the *corah* are *soron,* and *bolon*.

To make this instrument, Africans stretch a wet hide across the open side of a calabash and fasten it with lacing or pegs. They insert two round sticks lengthwise through the wet hide and one stick crosswise to support the central bridge over which the strings pass. When the hide dries, the entire top tightens. The eight strings are tied from the native fiber loop at the bottom to the fiber pieces which are wound around the neck of the instrument. The circular fiber pieces are raised or lowered to tighten or loosen the strings and thus change their pitches.

Bagwell and Miles

From Olatunji collection of African instruments

Lutes

The lute usually is shaped somewhat like the modern guitar and is played in similar fashion. It has a resonating body, a neck, and one or more strings which lie across the length of the body and neck of the instrument. The player tunes the strings by tightening or loosening the pegs at the top of the lute's neck.

All but four of these lutes[43] are from Mediterranean countries, for lutes are of Arab origin. Two examples of the *cambreh* or *halam* are from the west coast (475 and 473). Carved from a solid block of wood, the *cambreh* or *halam* has a membrane stretched over its open side and fastened to the edges with pegs. Its wooden neck pierces the membrane at the upper end of the body and passes through two slits just above the sound hole. Sometimes a metal rattle is attached to the upper part of the neck to add to the timbre. Three strings (of horsehair in 475, of gut in 473) pass over a small bridge to the bands of leather which are wound around the neck. The strings are plucked with a plectrum, sometimes made of an animal's tooth or a shell, thin piece of ivory or metal. The Ouloff people of Senegal call this instrument a *khalam*.

Two lutes are from the east coast (1659 and 483). The first of these, a *kouitara* or *kuitra* from Zanzibar, is a primitive instrument made from a half section of a bottle-shaped gourd with a neck and front of wood. The open peg box, bent backward slightly, has eight pegs. The four pairs of strings are played with a plectrum. Notice the similarity of this instrument to the *kuitra* from North Africa (495).

The second lute, an *icbacarre* (483) from Mozambique, illustrates once again that Africans make musical instruments from whatever materials are available. This interesting lute has a body made from a tin can. Its opening is covered with parchment held in place by small wooden pegs. The wooden neck has but one fiber string which is attached to the one tuning peg.

The *gaboussi* of the Malagasy Republic looks very much like instrument 1323 pictured here. It is made like the *kuitra*. The people of Mayette and Majunga use it for dances, festivals, and some of their rituals.

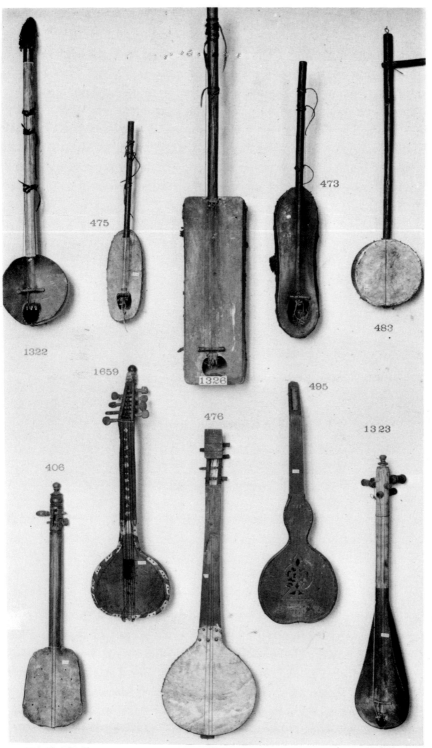

The Metropolitan Museum of Art, The Crosby Brown Collection of Musical Instruments, 1889

Zithers

Primitive zithers vary greatly in size and shape but all have their strings stretched along the body of the instrument. Unlike the lute, they have no neck. Some are played in an upright position and some are played horizontally. The modern zither consists of a flat resonating box which has a sound hole near the middle. Metal strings are stretched tightly across the box to a set of tuning pegs. The instrument, played horizontally, usually is placed on a table. The autoharp, so common in today's schools, is a zither with bars attached in such a way that depressing one at a time silences all the strings except those which will play a given chord when strummed. The autoharp has no sound hole. The zither is usually used to play melodies, while the autoharp is used to provide chords for singing.

The Metropolitan Museum of Art, The Crosby Brown Collection of Musical Instruments, 1889

Zithers,[44] common on both sides of the equator and south to the Zambesi River, are found also along the south coast of the western "bulge" of Africa. There are stick zithers, raft zithers, board zithers, trough zithers, and those which defy classification, like the one pictured above. This *marouvane* from Central Africa is made from the tail of a crocodile which forms an inverted shell. A skin is stretched over the hollow. The strings, supported by a wooden bridge, are plucked to accompany singing.

The white-haired Hutu tribesman of Rwanda plays an *inanga trough zither* as he recites the legends of his tribe. The construction of his instrument may be seen more clearly in the photograph which follows.

87

Trough zithers may be as shallow as the ones illustrated (513 and 515) or so deep that they appear to be as large as a baby's cradle. They are either rectangular or cylindrical in shape. A single string, laced back and forth through holes at either end, produces pleasant musical sounds when plucked. Sometimes these zithers have gourd resonators attached beneath to intensify and enrich their tones. In some parts of the Congo this instrument is known as a *marouvane* and in other parts, especially the former French Congo, it is called a *cithare*. The Bajandi tribesmen of Central Africa call it a *bandju* and the people of Tanganyika call it a *nanga zither* or a *ligombo zither*.

The two instruments at the left are raft zithers. Their similarity to a log raft is striking. These, of course, are much smaller and are made of cane, bamboo, or reed rather than of logs. The one at the top (410) is almost square, being one foot two inches long by ten and one-half inches wide. Its twenty bamboo tubes are fastened by the four tubes which cross them, forming bridges for the strings which are created in a unique manner. Slits are cut into the bamboo tubes and then pieces of the fiber are raised from the bamboo itself. The four cross tubes are slipped under these strings, thus creating a stringed instrument whose body, strings, and bridges are made from the same material.

A board zither, not illustrated here, is made by lacing a string through holes at both ends of a board and stretching it tightly over the two bridges which are placed at the ends. This type of zither often has a handle similar to those on the trough zithers described previously.

Two stick zithers are illustrated in the center of this photograph. The one at the bottom (553) is more primitive than the one with the palm-leaf hood (1489). These two *valihas* or *marouvanes* are from the Malagasy Republic. The simpler one, over four feet long, is held upright when played. Its strings are created in the same unique manner as those on the raft zither. Slits are cut into the bamboo tube and thin pieces of fiber are raised. Tiny bridges are slipped under the fiber strings so that the musician may pluck them to produce gentle, fascinating tones. The shorter *valiha,* almost two feet high, has twenty wire strings fastened to carved pegs. Its curved palm-leaf hood acts as a resonator.

Musicians in Gabon accompany themselves on an eight-stringed *valiha* which has a palm-leaf hood as they sing an epic tale of the heroic exploits of eight great warriors. Each string stands for the name of one of the warriors. Children are so impressed with musical events of this kind that even three- to five-year-olds make their own instruments spontaneously and sing in imitation of the adults.

The one instrument in this photograph which has not been described (1490) looks like a simple *valiha,* but is not one, for its strings are struck rather than plucked. Therefore, it is described in the next section.

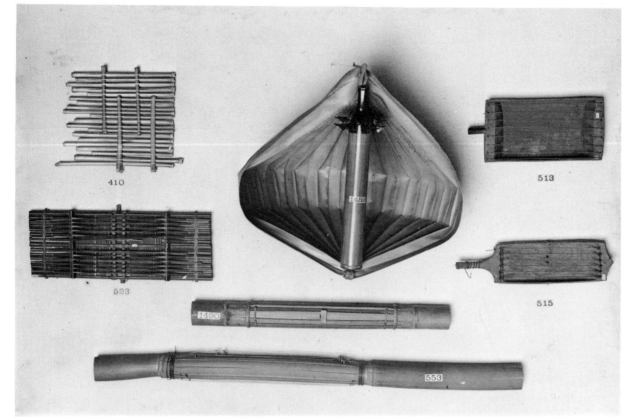

410

523

513

515

CHORDOPHONES WHOSE STRINGS ARE STRUCK

■   The instrument in the previous picture which looks like a stick zither is a dulcimer (1490). There is a small square opening in the center of the large bamboo tube which cannot be seen because a small piece of bark has been suspended across it. This little strip is held in place by two fiber strings cut from the surface of the tube and raised at either end by small wooden bridges. There is one additional string on each side. This dulcimer from the Malagasy Republic is identical with the *agong* of the Philippines. The strings are struck to produce musical tones.

Musical bows whose strings are struck by a stick, reed, wisp of straw, or tiny seed-shell rattle are classified as dulcimer-type chordophones. The Zulu *ntombazana* (young girl) pictured here holds the gourd resonator of her *ughubu* against her chest as she strikes the string with a thin reed. This photograph was taken at an agricultural show in Zululand where a man performed on a similar instrument called a *makweyana*. Zulu girls often play *ughubus* or *makweyanas* to accompany their singing as they go to parties. The Xhosa women of the Nguni tribes of the eastern seaboard of South Africa play a *hadi,* which looks something like the *ughubu,* when they sing their children to sleep.

■ Sometimes a musical bow not only provides melody, but a percussive accompaniment as well. Here we see a Shangaan tribesman of Mozambique playing the *chipendani mouth bow*. His bow is fitted with two rattles, gourds containing seeds, and the player holds a double rattle in his striking hand. His bow has a single string, stressed back near the center to produce two fundamental tones. The tones are produced by striking either segment of the string with a light stick and by plucking with the left first finger. He resonates the harmonics in his open mouth.

■ The musical bows[38] in the next picture, described in order from top to bottom, also are played by striking their strings. Thus, they are dulcimer-type chordophones. The first one has its string stretched from points a short distance from the ends of the bow. The ends curve upward. The bamboo tube which has been attached near the center acts as a resonator.

The second bow has a hole in the center of the back of the bow. The player beats the metal or cord string with a small twisted wire, seen below the bow. He places his mouth against the back of the bow over the hole to make the sound louder. By varying the tension of his lips, he can play five tones. The Kaffirs of Zululand, South Africa, play this *samuius* in their war and love songs, alternating the music of the bow with that of their singing.

The third bow, decorated with gay tassels, is played by Basuto tribesmen of Zululand. Notice that a flexible stick has been inserted into each end of a tube of bamboo. A single wire is stretched between the sticks. The loop of cord passing over the wire regulates its vibrating length and thus makes it possible for the player to change the pitch of this *tolo tolo*. He holds the bow to his mouth, thus using his mouth as a resonator, and taps the string with a stick. A smaller bow, similar in design, is called a *wedsa* in Mashonaland.

The fourth bow is the only one of this group which is used on the west coast and in the Congo region. The player places the open end of the gourd against his body and taps the hemp string with a small wisp of thatch much as the Zulu girl plays her *ughubu*. There is one important difference, however. This gourd is not firmly attached to the bow in one position like that on the *ughubu*. Notice that this resonating gourd is attached to the bow by means of a loop of cord which passes over the string. By slipping this gourd along the wooden bow the vibrating length of the string is regulated, and the musician can change the pitch of his playing. Why not make a musical bow like this and perform some experiments to discover the relationship between the length of a vibrating string and the pitch of the tone produced when the string is struck?

The *goura*, fifth from the top, is played by the Hottentots of South Africa. You cannot see the small wooden peg and the bit of flattened quill which are inserted about three and one-half inches from one end of the flexible rod of bamboo. The string is stretched between the quill on one end to the bamboo itself on the other end.

The sixth musical bow has an appearance totally unlike any of the others. A thin flexible stick is inserted into one end of a straight tube of bamboo. Between this stick and the opposite end of the bamboo tube a single fiber string is stretched. Below the bow we see two reed sticks, one of which is the striker and the other of which is used to regulate the tension of the string, thus changing the pitch of the music played.

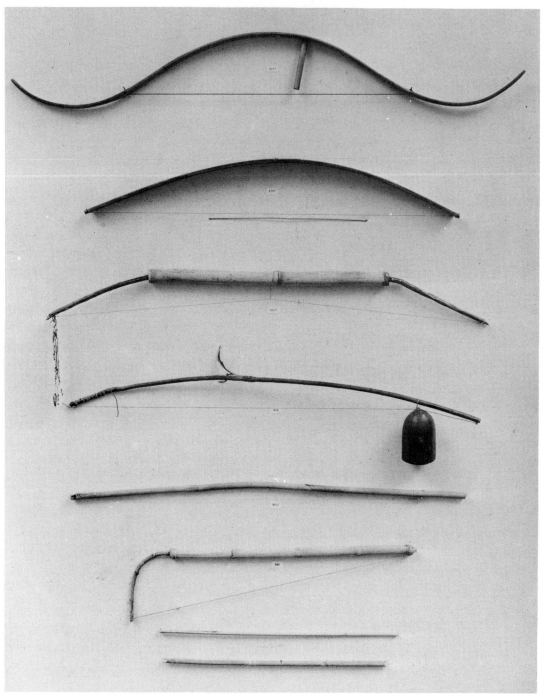

The Metropolitan Museum of Art, The Crosby Brown Collection of Musical Instruments, 1889

CHORDOPHONES WHOSE STRINGS ARE BOWED

■   Chordophones which are played with bows are more common in the Mediterranean region than in Africa south of the Sahara. However, some musical bows, such as the *chizembe friction bow* of Southern Rhodesia, and a number of rude fiddles are played throughout much of Africa except for the countries of the deep South. The bowed zither is found in Bechuanaland. Here we see a lad of the Tswana tribe playing the *segankuru bowed zither*. It is resonated by a tin attached to the top end. Long ago the resonator would have been a gourd.

■   The next photograph shows a man in French Guinea playing a *kalandin* made of a gourd with a wooden neck. The single string is bowed and there is one large sound hole in the body of the instrument.

■ Only three of the instruments in the next illustration are native to Africa south of the Sahara. The others are *rebabs* and *kemangehs* from the Islamic countries of the north coast. The *koundyeh* or *ngiemeh* from Sierra Leone pictured in the bottom row (477) is a primitive fiddle made from a coconut shell. Its opening is covered with lizard skin in which there is one large sound hole. The single horsehair string is bound to the top of the round, straight, wooden neck by a band of leather. It is attached to the opposite end by a loop of cord. The arched bow made of natural wood and horsehair is ornamented with metal rings.

The two instruments on the left and right ends of the bottom row (3320 and 3319) which look like rude violins[45] are *kakoshis*. Both have bodies carved from blocks of wood. The one on the right has its open side covered with a thin board into which a number of small sound holes have been pierced. Each instrument has a long straight neck of round wood and a large open peg box with three pegs. Each *kakoshi* also has three strings fastened to the lower edge of the instrument by means of two cords. Men of the Masango tribe of Angola play the *kakoshi* with a bow.

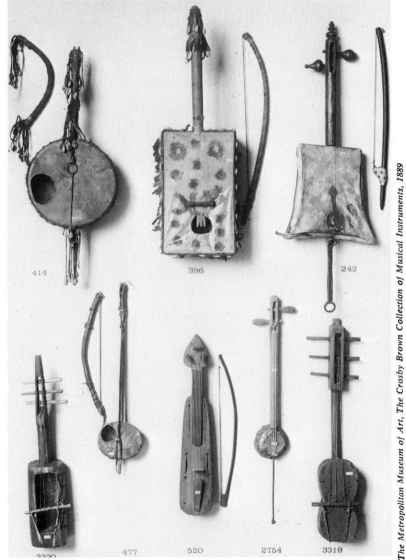

414   396   242

3320   477   520   2754   3319

96

■   Once again we see that music plays a significant part in the ceremonies honoring influential guests. These musicians play a gourd rattle and a tube fiddle. The body of the fiddle appears to be made from a gourd. Members of the United Nations Visiting Mission to Trust Territories in West Africa were leaving Bimbilla area, British Togoland. The United Nations Trusteeship Council had sent this group to visit the Cameroons and Togoland under French administration and the Cameroons and Togoland under British administration.   These territories became the independent nations of Cameroon and Togo in 1960.

Tube fiddles of this type are found all across Africa from Guinea to Uganda and Kenya. The body of the fiddle may be made of a gourd, a tin can, or a hollowed block of wood. If a membrane is stretched across its open top, it is fastened with pegs or tacks. A tassel of goat's hair or woven fiber frequently adds gay decoration to the round wooden neck which goes all the way through the body of the fiddle. Notice how small the bow of this instrument is.

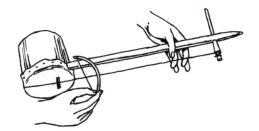

■   These four members of the Ganda tribe of Uganda make up a typical band of musicians. The first man plays a *kihembe ngoma* which was described in the chapter on Membranophones. The third player holds his *kissar,* a lyre whose strings he plucks. The second and fourth musicians play *tube fiddles,* lutes whose strings are bowed. Notice the gay decorations, the small bows, and the way in which each musician places his hands on his instrument. Bands such as these play for all kinds of festive occasions.

EPILOGUE

■   Winds of change blow over Africa. In some places the force is that of a hurricane, in others it has slowed to a gale, and in a very few places its tempo has dropped to a breeze. Colonialism is disappearing. Many new nations have been born and admitted to the United Nations. Cities are gradually being industrialized and Westernized. Rural Africa, clinging to ancient tribal traditions, changes more slowly. In this process of change, Africans must not lose their great cultural heritage nor their spirit.

Change is not new to Africa. According to modern archaeologists, the Africa we know and the one which existed only a few decades ago is not the Africa of long ago. Most schoolchildren study the highly developed civilization of ancient Egypt, but few children or their parents know that today's scientists have recently discovered evidence that there were many other civilizations in Africa as highly developed as that of Egypt. These ranged from the shores of the Mediterranean to the Cape of Good Hope.

Leo Frobenius reported that the explorers of the fifteenth and sixteenth centuries found a beautiful city with fine buildings and tree-lined streets on the shores of the Bay of Guinea. Its people were dressed in rich silks and velvets. The explorers conquered the people and pressed them into slavery. In order to justify their actions, they treated the African slaves as animals. "The notion of the 'black savage' is a European invention" which people believed up to the beginning of the twentieth century, the archaeologist wrote.

African slaves brought their music to the shores of North America and soon Negro spirituals and jazz were born. Modern composers of serious music used the strange chords, the complicated rhythms, the "blue" notes, and percussion of jazz in the music they wrote. Thus, modern symphonic music, growing from jazz which has its roots in Africa, owes much to African music. Today even the music of the Catholic Church is responding to African music. Late in 1962 an African Mass was celebrated in the great church of St. Peter in Rome. The Mass was based on an old Ethiopian ritual which dates back to the fourth century. Just as much of African music is based on a call-and-response pattern carried on between a leader and the people, so this Mass is based on a similar pattern of chanting between the priest and the congregation. African instruments —drums and bells—were played in complex rhythms, and the people clapped their hands rhythmically, too. Never before had such vibrant, rhythmic sounds been heard in St. Peter's. One priest commented, "St. Peter's was jumping, in a dignified sort of way." The Christian African of today, like the traditional tribal African, expresses his religion vigorously through music. Many Catholic Fathers have urged that portions of the Mass be said, not in Latin, but in the language of the people. Now that this is possible, new African Masses will surely appear. Thus, we see that African music exerts a powerful influence on the music of the world.

The music of the Western world now threatens to destroy the traditional music of Africa. Jazz, jive, and rock 'n' roll spread throughout the continent. Young people abandon the native instruments and play guitars to accompany singing. So widespread has this become that in 1961 some professional musicians in Kenya requested Europeans to make a rule against guitar playing.

In some places, however, the old music remains. Even in these places the instruments are changing somewhat. Gong-gongs are made, not only of metal, but also from discarded bottles. Rattles are made from the caps of Coca-Cola bottles. Gasoline cans are fashioned into drums. The metal stays of discarded umbrellas are made into tongues for thumb pianos. Enterprising Africans continue to make musical instruments of anything and everything.

The winds of change which blow over Africa must not be allowed to destroy her cultural heritage. Her music, her dances, her artistic masks, and her ways of living express the people's great faith, their spiritual quality. Africans and Westerners are working together to preserve the rich musical tradition. For instance, when African musicians from all over Kenya came together in 1961, Westerners recorded their playing and singing, made photographs, and took notes on the construction, tuning, and method of playing each instrument. This traditional music will not be lost!

Extensive studies of African culture have been made only during the past thirty years or so. They indicate that there is a great deal still to be learned about musical instruments, the varied rhythms and melodies, the kind of scale used, whether or not African music has harmony, and the place of music in the life of the people. Old rituals, songs, and dances must be preserved for the children of the future. African music is not yet understood by the Westerner; it must be rediscovered by the African and made a part of the education of his children. Some modern Africans, educated in the United States or Europe, even plan the development of great cultural centers where the art, music, and dance of their countries may always be seen and heard.

We who are interested in African music and African musical instruments must preserve the knowledge we have and encourage further investigation. The whole world will be richer if traditional forms of music and dance are not lost, if African and Western musical forms intermingle, and if the influences which create change in both directions serve to stimulate musicians to develop new musical forms.

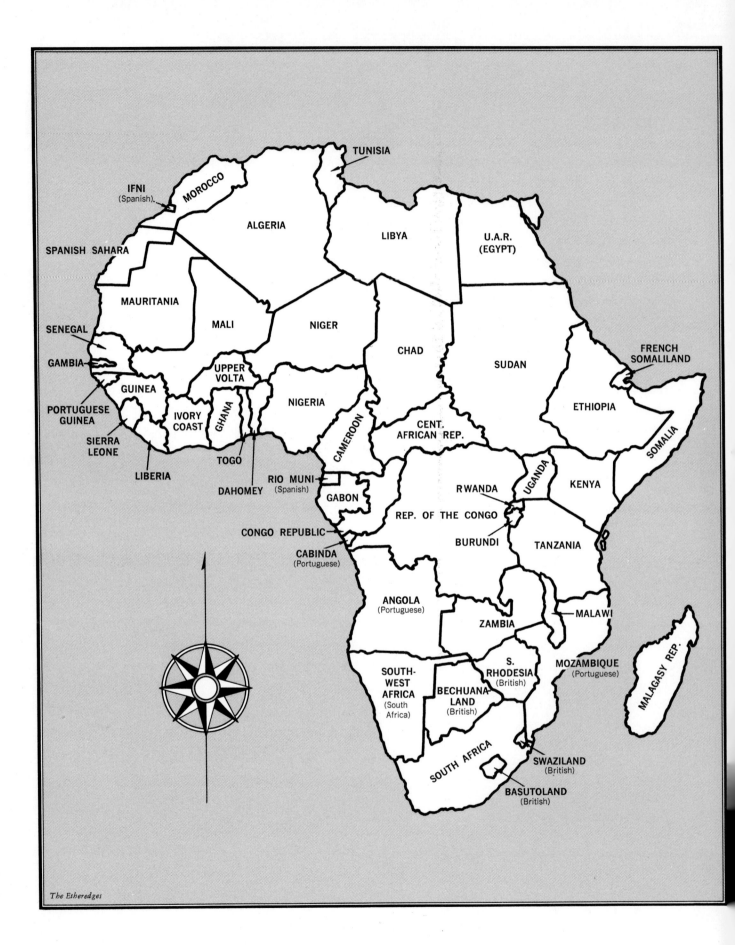

TUNISIA

IFNI
(Spanish)

MOROCCO

ALGERIA

LIBYA

U.A.R.
(EGYPT)

SPANISH SAHARA

MAURITANIA

MALI

NIGER

CHAD

SUDAN

SENEGAL

FRENCH
SOMALILAND

GAMBIA

UPPER
VOLTA

GUINEA

PORTUGUESE
GUINEA

IVORY
COAST

GHANA

NIGERIA

ETHIOPIA

SIERRA
LEONE

TOGO

CAMEROON

CENT.
AFRICAN REP.

SOMALIA

LIBERIA

DAHOMEY

RIO MUNI
(Spanish)

GABON

REP. OF THE CONGO

UGANDA

RWANDA

KENYA

CONGO REPUBLIC

BURUNDI

TANZANIA

CABINDA
(Portuguese)

ANGOLA
(Portuguese)

MALAWI

ZAMBIA

MOZAMBIQUE
(Portuguese)

MALAGASY REP.

SOUTH-
WEST
AFRICA
(South
Africa)

BECHUANA-
LAND
(British)

S.
RHODESIA
(British)

SOUTH AFRICA

SWAZILAND
(British)

BASUTOLAND
(British)

The Etheredges

102

TO PARENTS AND TEACHERS

■   The countries of Africa are destined to become increasingly important in world affairs. No longer can we permit ourselves to be uninformed or misinformed about that great continent. In order to eradicate the many stereotypes and to promote a sincere appreciation of her culture, we must seek out facts. Since most people have a healthy curiosity about Africa, it should not be difficult to stimulate their search for the most up-to-date information available about her rapidly changing political divisions, social conditions, and her arts.

Map and globe study thrill many children. Compare African maps of 1945 with those of 1955 and the present. Study the list of *The Independent Nations of Africa,* which follows this section, to discover in which year the largest number of independent states was born. Colonialism's retreat in Africa has been rapid, and the membership of the United Nations has grown as quickly.

The study of the political changes can be linked to discussions about what other changes probably are taking place. What is happening to tribal life? How are urbanization and industrialization affecting African life? What modifications are taking place in the peoples' basic values and beliefs? Does all Africa still sing, dance, and play musical instruments spontaneously?

Worthwhile rhythmic activities for young children grow from careful observation of African animals in zoos or in films. Youngsters walk like elephants, slink like leopards stalking their prey, lumber as clumsily as rhinoceroses, or leap as gracefully as gazelles. The adult who plays a tom-tom to follow the rhythm set by the child encourages individual creative responses.

A search for ways to make instruments similar to those illustrated leads to exploration of the science of sound production and reception. The directions for making the *sakara* are explicit. Study the illustrations and descriptions of other instruments to discover ways to make them from tin cans, barrels, and other materials. Then play them. The enjoyment of this kind of experience knows no age limit. Even the members of the Chicago Symphony Orchestra once played a concert on improvised instruments made from kitchen utensils, washboards, and other household items.*

People of all ages gain satisfaction from listening to African music. Older children exhibit interest in comparing authentic field recordings with the popular music of today's urban Africa — that which shows evidences of acculturation. It fascinates them, also, to compare the music of Africa with African-influenced North American folk music and jazz.

African arts and crafts have great appeal for American children. If possible take them to an exhibit. Show them photographs of the arts of the many tribes. Then encourage them to make art objects of similar materials.

The most valuable experience of all is to become acquainted with African people. Invite citizens of African countries to visit you. Share experiences — and music — with each other. Develop friendships. In this manner, we may one day learn to become sensitive to the values held by Africa's many peoples and thus gain the kind of mutual appreciation which is the basis of world peace.

* The author remembers with pleasure an invitational concert played many years ago by the members of this august body of musicians. Attired in white aprons and chef's hats, they appeared to be even more delighted than the enthusiastic audience.

THE INDEPENDENT NATIONS OF AFRICA

NAME OF COUNTRY	DATE OF INDEPENDENCE	DATE OF U.N. MEMBERSHIP
Algeria	July 3, 1962	Oct. 8, 1962
Burundi	July 1, 1962	Sept. 18, 1962
Cameroon	Jan. 1, 1960	Sept. 20, 1960
Central African Republic	Aug. 13, 1960	Sept. 20, 1960
Chad	Aug. 11, 1960	Sept. 20, 1960
Congo-Brazzaville	Aug. 15, 1960	Sept. 20, 1960
Congo-Leopoldville	June 30, 1960	Sept. 20, 1960
Dahomey	Aug. 1, 1960	Sept. 20, 1960
Ethiopia	Since Biblical Days	Nov. 13, 1945
Gabon	Aug. 17, 1960	Sept. 20, 1960
Ghana	Mar. 6, 1957	Mar. 8, 1957

Guinea	Oct. 2, 1958	Dec. 12, 1958
Ivory Coast	Aug. 7, 1960	Sept. 20, 1960
Kenya	Dec. 12, 1963	Dec. 16, 1963
Liberia	1847	Nov. 2, 1945
Libya	Dec. 24, 1951	Dec. 14, 1955
Malagasy Republic	June 26, 1960	Sept. 20, 1960
Malawi	July 6, 1964	Dec. 1, 1964
Mali	Sept. 22, 1960	Sept. 28, 1960
Mauritania	Nov. 28, 1960	Oct. 27, 1961
Morocco	Mar. 2, 1956	Nov. 12, 1956
Niger	Aug. 3, 1960	Sept. 20, 1960
Nigeria	Oct. 1, 1960	Oct. 7, 1960
Rwanda	July 1, 1962	Sept. 18, 1962
Senegal	Aug. 20, 1960	Sept. 28, 1960
Sierra Leone*	Apr. 27, 1961	Sept. 27, 1961
Somalia	July 1, 1960	Sept. 20, 1960
South Africa	May 31, 1910	Nov. 7, 1945
Sudan	Jan. 1, 1956	Nov. 12, 1956
Tanzania	Dec. 9, 1961	Dec. 14, 1961
Togo	April 27, 1960	Sept. 20, 1960
Tunisia	Mar. 20, 1956	Nov. 12, 1956
Uganda	Oct. 9, 1962	Oct. 25, 1962
United Arab Republic**	1922	Oct. 24, 1945
Upper Volta	Aug. 5, 1960	Sept. 20, 1960
Zambia	Oct. 24, 1964	Dec. 1, 1964

*   Sierra Leone was the 100th nation to join the United Nations.

**   Egypt was an original member of the United Nations. On February 21, 1958, Egypt and Syria joined forces and became the United Arab Republic. Syria withdrew from the Union and resumed its independent status on Oct. 31, 1961, again having its own membership in the United Nations.

Gambia (British) is due to be granted independence Feb. 18, 1965.

NOTES ABOUT THE INSTRUMENTS PLAYED ON THE RECORD IN THE BACK OF THIS BOOK

MEMBRANOPHONES

■ 1. EWE (Ghana/Togo) *agbadza* dance: Drum orchestra with gong-gong and rattle. The accompanying dance re-enacts a legendary battle between two armies, the dancers are armed with wooden swords. The master drum is free to improvise against the fixed rhythms of the other drums.

IDIOPHONES

■ 2. BaMBUTI Pygmies, Ituri Forest, Congo. Percussion sticks. These people virtually have no musical instruments except for the musical bow and two types of percussion sticks. One type, *banza,* is shaved at the ends and either tapped on a log or stroked together; the other, *ngbengbe,* is merely short sticks stripped of bark, notched to give the correct tone and pitch, and beaten together. The *ngbengbe,* as heard here, always and only accompany honey-gathering songs.

■ 3. BaNDAKA, N. E. Congo. Slit gong. Logs of almost any size, from ten inches to ten feet in length, are hollowed out and used as signal gongs for sending messages. This small *mgungu* gong is being used to call villagers together. It may also be used as accompaniment to dance.

■ 4. ACOLI: Uganda. Xylophone. Some African xylophones have gourds attached as resonators, but in this case slabs of wood, acting as the keys, are simply laid across two stems of banana trees, and are struck by two players. Although no song accompanies this performance, it is known and recognized as telling a tribal legend. It is therefore a means of reinforcing tribal values, as well as being an instrument of pleasure.

■ 5. BaNGWANA: N. E. Congo. "Hand piano." Known by many names, particularly *sanza* in East Africa; in this region known as *lukembi,* this is probably the most common instrument south of the Sahara, and is uniquely African. It is made simply of a piece of wood, sometimes hollowed out, sometimes set in a gourd (as resonator), on top of which a number of bamboo or metal (as in this case) tongues are attached over a bridge, and plucked with the thumbs.

AEROPHONES

■ 6. BaBIRA: N. E. Congo. Trumpet. Made of the ivory tusk of an elephant, bored for side-blowing, the trumpet is used for signaling. Antelope horns are also used, and gourds and wood. In the latter two cases trumpets of different pitch are sometimes used in concert to accompany dances.

■ 7. BaMBUTI Pygmies, Congo. Flute. Although this is not a Pygmy instrument, the Pygmies are perfectly capable of playing it, as well as other instruments. This one was cut from a reed on the spot, the stop holes burned with a smouldering stick of wood. After playing it was thrown away. It is end-blown.

■ 8. BaBIRA: N. E. Congo. Flute orchestra. A series of notched, end-blown single-pitch pipes, cut from different lengths of bamboo, are combined and played in *hoquet.* This flute orchestra is used particularly to accompany a group of youths dancing their way to a neighboring village to court girls.

CHORDOPHONES

■ 9. ACOLI: Uganda. Harp. Derived from the musical bow, many harps in Africa, such as this one, retain the basic shape of the bow, with a boat-shaped wooden resonator fixed to one end. The five strings pass from the head of the bow, where they are tightened by pegs, to the top of the resonator, which is covered with bark or, as here, snakeskin. The song tells of a tribal legend, and as with the xylophone is a means of both giving pleasure and of reinforcing tribal values.

■ 10. BaBIRA: N. E. Congo. Zither. Used for personal pleasure, or, as here, to make a long foot-journey through the forest less tedious. Some zithers are made of tubes of bamboo, some of troughs hollowed out of hard wood, but this one is a simple wooden board, a twig at each end acting as a bridge, with a length of vine wound around to give twelve strings. These strings are raised farther from the board by small bamboo pegs, and can be tuned by moving these pegs. The thumbs are used to pluck the strings.

Recordings made in Africa by Colin M. Turnbull, Assistant Curator, in charge of African Ethnology at the American Museum of Natural History in New York City. Program notes written by Colin Turnbull, also.

LIST OF RECORDINGS

Music of the Falashas, Folkways   5, 16, 40
Music of the Ituri Forest People, Folkways   2, 15, 22, 27, 31, 33, 38
Olatunji, Drums of Passion, Columbia   4, 13, 16, 20, 23
Olatunji, Flaming Drums, Columbia   3, 7
Songs of the Congo, Epic   6
Topeke People of the Congo, Folkways   9, 15, 25, 38, 44
Voice of the Congo, Washington   10, 14, 44

*   See also the other African recordings in the Ethnic Folkways Library.

BOOKS FOR FURTHER READING

ALLEN, WILLIAM D., *Africa*. Grand Rapids, Michigan: The Fideler Company, 1964

BUCKLEY, PETER, *Okolo of Nigeria*. New York: Simon and Schuster, Inc., 1962

CALDWELL, JOHN C., *Let's Visit West Africa*. New York: The John Day Co., 1959

CALDWELL, JOHN C., *Our Neighbors in Africa*. New York: The John Day Co., 1961

GATTI, ELLEN M., *The New Africa*. New York: Scribner's Sons, 1960

GUNTHER, JOHN, *Meet the Congo and Its Neighbors*. New York: Harper and Brothers, 1959

HUGHES, LANGSTON, *The First Book of Africa*. New York: Franklin Watts, 1960

KENWORTHY, LEONARD S., *Profile of Nigeria*. Garden City: Doubleday and Co., 1960

KITTLER, GLENN, *Equatorial Africa: The New World of Tomorrow*. Garden City: Nelson Doubleday, 1959

LANDECK, BEATRICE, *Echoes of Africa in Folk Songs of the Americas*. New York: David McKay Co., 1961

RADIN, PAUL, and SWEENEY, JAMES J., selected by, *African Folk Tales and Sculpture.* New York: Pantheon Books, 1952

ROHRBAUGH, LYNN, ed., *African Songs.* Delaware, Ohio: Cooperative Recreation Service, 1958 (30¢)

SAVAGE, KATHARINE, *The Story of Africa South of the Sahara.* New York: Henry Z. Walck, 1961

SCHULTHESS, EMIL, *Africa.* New York: Simon and Schuster, 1959

SUTHERLAND, EFUA, *Playtime in Africa.* New York: Atheneum, 1962

TURNBULL, COLIN M., *The Peoples of Africa.* New York: World Publishing Co., 1962

WRIGHT, ROSE, *Fun and Festival From Africa.* Friendship Press, 1958 (75¢)

ADDITIONAL BOOKS FOR ADULTS

DAVIDSON, BASIL, *The Lost Cities of Africa*. Boston: Little, Brown and Co., 1959

DINESEN, ISAK, *Out of Africa*. New York: Modern Library, 1952

GOLDSCHMIDT, WALTER, ed., *United States and Africa*. New York: Praeger, 1963

HEMPSTONE, SMITH, *Africa: Angry Young Giant*. New York: Frederick A. Praeger, 1961

HUGHES, LANGSTON, *Poems From Black Africa*. Bloomington, Indiana: Indiana University Press, 1963

KENWORTHY, LEONARD S., *Studying Africa in Elementary and Secondary Schools*. New York: Bureau of Publications, Teachers College, Columbia University, 1965

TOOZE, RUTH, and KRONE, BEATRICE, *Music and Literature as Resources for the Social Studies*. Englewood Cliffs, New Jersey: Prentice-Hall, 1955

TURNBULL, COLIN M., *The Forest People*. New York: Simon and Schuster, Inc., 1961

TURNBULL, COLIN M., *The Lonely African*. New York: Simon and Schuster, Inc., 1962

VAN DER POST, LAURENS, *The Heart of the Hunter*. New York: William Morrow and Co., Inc., 1961

VAN DER POST, LAURENS, *Venture to the Interior*. New York: William Morrow and Co., Inc., 1951

GUIDE TO PRONUNCIATION

agbe—ah gbeh
agidibo—ah GEE di boh
ahatse—ah ha TSEH
akam—ah KAHM
angra ocwena—ahng grah oh KWEH nah
antsiva—ahn TCHEE vah
asiwui—ah SHEE vwee
asukusuk—ah SOO koo sook
atenesu—ah TEHN eh soo
atoke—ah TOH keh
atsimevu—ah TCHEE meh vwoo
azoey—ah ZOH way
bandju—bahn JOO
baragumu—bah rah GOO moo
bata—bah TAH
bembe—behm beh
bolon—boh LUN
cambreh—kam BRAY
chebab—chee bab
chipendani—chee pehn DAH nee
chizambe—chee ZAM beh
chisanza mbira—chee SAHN zah m BEE rah
chizembe—chee ZEM beh
cithare—see TAH reh
colangee—koh lan GEE
conga—KOHNG gah
corah—koh RAH
djouwak—DJOH wak
dundun—doohm DOOHN
efumbu—eh foom BU
eleke—eh LEH keh
ennanga—ehn NAHNG gah
endonyi—ehn DOOHN yee
entenga—ehn TEHNG gah
epele—eh PEH leh
gaboussi—gah BOO see
gangan—gahng GAHNG
gankogui—gahn KOH gwee
gambareh—gahm BAH reh
goura—goo rah
gubo—goo boh
gugudu—goo goo DOO
hadi—hah DEE
halam—hah LAHM
herrauou—heh RAH woo
hova—hoh VAH
ichacarre—ik BAH kah reh
igbin—ig BIN
ilukere—i loo KEH reh
inanga—ee NAHNG gah

ingqonqo—ing KONG koh
insimbi—in sim BEE
iya igbin—ee YAH ig BIN
iya ilu—ee YAH ee loo
jagba—jah gBAH
kaffir—kah feer
kaganj—KAH gahng
kakaki—kah KAH kee
kakoshis—ka KOH sheez
kalandin—kah lahn DIN
kalimbre mbira—kah LIM beh m BEE rah
kanango—kah nang GOH
kanih—kah NEE
kasayi—kah sah YEE
kasso—kah soh
kehembe ngoma—kee HEM beh n GOH mah
kemanzeh—kee MAHN jehz
kembe—KEHM beh
khalam—kah LAHM
kidi—kee DEE
kihembe—kee HEHM beh
kinanda—kee NAHN dah
kerikeri—KEH ri KEH ri
kisanji—kee SAHNG ee
kissars—kee SAHR
kora—koh RAH
kouitara—kwee TAH rah
koundyeh—koon DYEH
kudi—koo DEE
kuitra—kwee trah
kundi—koon DEE
ligombo—lee gohm boh
lilolo—LEE loh loh
lokanga—loh KAHNG gah
lukembe—loo KEHM beh
madinda—mah DEEN dah
maduimba—mah doo EEM bah
makaji—mah kah GEE
makweyana—mah kwā YANA
malimba mbira—mah LIM bah m BEE rah
malimbe—mah LIM beh
malipenga—mah lee PEHNG gah
malume—mah loo meh
mare—mah reh
marimba—mah RIM bah
marouvane—mah roo VAHN eh
masonguo—mah SOHNG kwoh
mbira—m BEE rah
mbira huru—m BEE rah HOO roo
mishiba—mee SHEE bah

moropa—moh ROH pah
muet—myoo eht
murumbu—moo ROOM boo
nanga—NAHNG gah
ndere—n DEH reh
ngiemeh—n GEE meh
ngoma—n GOH mah
n'goms—n'GOHMZ
ngonge—n GOHNG djeh
njara mbira—n JAH rah m BEE rah
ntara—n TAH rah
ntimbo—n TIM boh
ntombazana—n TOHM bah ZAH na
obah—oh BAH
ogororo—oh GOH roh roh
olwet—ohl weh
ombi—ohm BEE
omele—oh MAY lay
omele abo—oh MAY lay ah BOH
omele ako—oh MAY lay ah KOH
omuhoro—oh moo HOH roh
oopoochawa—oo pooh CHAH wah
pluriare—ploo ree AH reh
rebahs—REE bahbz
sakara—SAH ka rah
sansa—SAHN sah
samuius—sah moo YOOS
segankuru—seh JAN koo roo
shaworo—shah woh ROH
shekere—SHEH keh reh
shona mbira—SHOH nah m BEE rah
siwa—see WAH
sogo—so go
soron—so RUN
Tabala—tah bah lah
Tambour—tam BOOR
Tolotolo—toh loh toh loh
tzetze—tzeh tzeh
ughubu—oog HOO boo
uluru—oo loo ROO
umuguri—oo moo GOO ri
valga—vahl gah
valiha—vah LEE ha
voatava—vwo hah TAH vah
wambee—wam BEE
wedsa—weh dsah
yatta yatta—yah tah yah tah
yayatsena—yah yah TSEH nah
Zanza—ZAHN zah
Zeze—zeh zeh

115

ABOUT THE AUTHORS

■   A graduate of Northwestern University, Dr. Betty Warner Dietz received her doctorate in education at New York University, has taught in public schools in Scarsdale, New York, New Orleans and Deerfield, Illinois, and since 1950 at Brooklyn College, where she now works in the capacity of associate professor.

Dr. Dietz visited Africa with her family when she was fifteen years old and since that time has had a great interest in the music of that continent.

Dr. Dietz has written book reviews and articles in *School Library Journal, Journal of Teacher Education, Childhood Education,* etc. Recently published by The John Day Company is her book *Folk Songs of China, Japan, Korea,* written with Thomas Choonbai Park. Her next book is to be about the musical instruments of Asia.

Michael Babatunde Olatunji, a Nigerian, was graduated from Morehouse College, Atlanta, Georgia and is currently a candidate for a Ph.D. degree in Public Administration at New York University. He has been presenting African music in lecture recitals at schools and universities all over the United States of America, and enjoys great popularity. He records for Columbia and Roulette Records, and has appeared on many television shows.